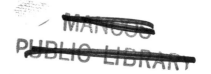

The Library Administration Series

Lowell A. Martin, General Editor

1. Alex Ladenson, *Library Law and Legislation in the United States,* 1982
2. R. Kathleen Molz, *Library Planning and Policy Making,* 1990
3. Donald J. Sager, *Participatory Management in Libraries,* 1982
5. Lowell A. Martin, *Organizational Structure of Libraries,* 1984
6. Norman Stevens, *Communication Throughout Libraries,* 1983
8. Ann E. Prentice, *Financial Planning for Libraries,* 2nd ed., 1995
9. Raymond M. Holt, *Planning Library Buildings and Facilities: From Concept to Completion,* 1989
10. Cosette Kies, *Marketing and Public Relations for Libraries,* 1987
11. Lowell A. Martin, *Library Personnel Administration,* 1994

FINANCIAL PLANNING FOR LIBRARIES
Second Edition

Ann E. Prentice

The Library Administration Series, No. 8

The Scarecrow Press, Inc.
Lanham, Md., & London

SCARECROW PRESS, INC.

Published in the United States of America
by Scarecrow Press, Inc.
4720 Boston Way
Lanham, Maryland 20706

4 Pleydell Gardens, Folkestone
Kent CT20 2DN, England

British Cataloguing-in-Publication Information Available

Library of Congress Cataloging-in-Publication Data

Prentice, Ann E.
Financial planning for libraries / by Ann E. Prentice.—2nd ed.
p. cm.—(The Library administration series ; no. 8)
Includes bibliographical referencs and index.
1. Library finance—United States. I. Title. II. Series:
Scarecrow library administration series ; no. 8.
Z683.2.U6P74 1996 025.1'1—dc20 94–42908

ISBN 0-8108-2974-6 (cloth : alk. paper)

CONTENTS

PREFACE TO THE SECOND EDITION

In this new edition, Dr. Prentice retains the underlying principles which distinguished her earlier volume: the impact of the economic environment on libraries, the interrelations of financial and service planning, thorough attention to budgeting, and realistic appraisal of the prospects for the support of libraries. To this foundation she adds the economic and governmental base of the 1990s and the impact of new technology and the emerging information infrastructure, right down to Internet and the 1994 National Telecommunications and Information Administration (NTIA), and she discerns hopeful prospects along the Information Highway.

Dr. Prentice first takes a broad look at the environment in which financial planning must perforce take place. Her early discussion deals with political, economic, and technological trends and their impact on library appropriations and expenditures. She urges library administrators to develop sensitivity to such trends, asserting that "to do less is to be an accountant rather than a library planner."

Also in accord with her basic approach is the considerable attention Dr. Prentice gives to newer budget forms—performance, program, zero-base—that stress the foundation of planning. Such emphasis leads in turn to examinations of financial measurement and accountability.

The techniques of financial planning are here, for gathering data, for analyzing costs, for controlling expenditures. The author covers the intriguing topic of cost/benefit analysis, with recognition of the difficulty of objectively determining the individual or social value of library services. A whole chapter is devoted to sources of income and the seeking of appropriations.

In the end Dr. Prentice takes a look ahead at financial prospects. She does not take the easy way out, of basing the future on state and federal monetary aid. Rather the emphasis is on better financial planning to get the maximum return from resources available. The tone of this book is at once forward-looking and realistic.

v

All this is consistent with the general purpose of the Scarecrow series on library administration. The aim is to help librarians who have become or will become administrators to understand and to apply modern management philosophies and methods.

Dr. Prentice was a public-library director herself before going on to take her doctorate at Columbia University. Her dissertation probed the delicate area of trustee contribution—or lack of contribution—to the financial support of public libraries. She went on to the faculties of two library schools, most recently as head of such a unit and therefore a participant in financial planning at the university level. Along the way she started and edited the *Public Library Quarterly,* a research journal, and published in the field of her particular expertise, that of library finance.

Lowell A. Martin
Series Editor

I.

THE ENVIRONMENT FOR
FINANCIAL PLANNING

Financial planning for library and information services is carried out in a complex environment. Past and present trends outside the library affect budget planning as much as or more than any internal cost analyses or dollar figures. Effective administrators are sensitive to these forces and learn to interact with and anticipate the wider scene—to do less is to be an accountant rather than a library planner.

This environment is the product of an ever-changing continuum of political, economic, and technological activities. The structures within an organization and within local, state and national government are an additional variable. Finally, the clienteles themselves, as they change and as their demands and expectations evolve, strongly affect library planning. Like other service organizations, libraries are dependent on all of these factors.

Given these broad conditions, library administrators proceed to make decisions based on current and past practice. But events do not stand still; new developments occur even in the course of a budget year and call for adjustments. Decisions are further modified by how the staff perceives the success of its efforts. Often the external environments do not appear to staff to be nearly as important as internal conditions and programs.

Also to be considered are professional standards and pressures. The library and information professions each have the trappings of educational objectives, service expectations, and operational objectives. Each is growing and changing rapidly, in large part in response to opportunities afforded by massive technological advances. Those technological advances, in turn, have resulted in new ways of looking at how organizations are organized and operate. Change also results from increased recognition by government and business officials of the value of reliable information and the need for advanced skills to organize and maintain the information.

These environments—external, internal, and professional—have an impact upon the decision-making process in libraries and often are in opposition. For example, professional considerations may run afoul of political or economic considerations. Standards set by professional agencies for library service may exceed the funds the political representatives are willing to provide. Traditional organizational structures may limit efficiency but staff may find that changing them is unsettling. Technological innovation may occur more rapidly than staff are willing to assimilate it.

It is not the purpose of this introduction to identify all possible elements within which financial planning takes place or all of the conflicts between and among these environmental demands. However, the following review of the principal factors and their impact on library service should be helpful in clarifying the way in which financial planning takes place.

THE CURRENT ENVIRONMENT

Following the 1960s, a period of rapid growth and great upheaval, have been years of assimilation of some of the social and economic changes and rejection of others. The 1970s were a sobering time in which inflation ate at the economic health of the country and the realization that we were no longer self-sufficient in a number of basic resources was damaging both to pride and the pocket book. Economically, the decades of the 1970s, 1980s and into the 1990s were a period of slow growth. Support for libraries and library service during this period ranged from very slow growth, to steady state, to decline.

As we move into the era of global economy, the self-sufficiency of an earlier day is no longer a possibility. Rather than dealing with individual European countries we now deal also with the European Common Market. The North American Free Trade Agreement (NAFTA) links us more closely with our continental neighbors. As similar agreements are developed elsewhere in the world, our economy and the accompanying role of information will continue to change from one of independence to one of interdependence. The restructuring of business and industry to meet new challenges has resulted in major changes in many of our largest companies.

Technology has allowed us to change the configuration of both manufacturing and service industries by automating processes, improving quality and at the same time reducing the number of employees necessary to run an operation. The increasing sophistication of management information systems and the ability to generate and massage information electronically for decision-making has reduced the need for some clerical and middle management positions and has thus flattened the organization. The new lean and mean organization is smaller yet more productive than the organizational configuration it replaced.

New skills are needed to make the newly structured organizations function well. A result of the massive restructuring of the way in which business and industry operate is that a mismatch has developed between skills needed and skills available. Those who have embraced the new technology and grown along with it have been able to make the transition, but those whose skills are outdated have found that they have limited employment futures. In a period of slow growth and a period in which many employers are reducing their permanent workforce, additional social and educational services are necessary to support the jobless as they make a transition into the newly configuring economy.

To a degree, information is exempt from the conflicting views of political interests. It is seen as an important element in decision making and is in itself unbiased. The ownership of information and the uses to which it is put are entirely different matters. The development of national and international information networks and federal support of a national information infrastructure have placed information, its access and use, in the forefront of national planning. Decisions as to how we build our information infrastructure, who finances it, who has access to it and how we use it are among the most important decisions of the next decade.

POLITICAL FACTORS IN THE ENVIRONMENT

Libraries are funded as a result of political decisions made in an environment much broader than that of the library. Overall policy and fiscal policy are determined by citizens and their elected representatives. Voters and local, state, and federal government decision-makers set the broad policy outlines for publicly funded institutions, including libraries. This is the case for the public library, the public academic library, libraries of government agencies at all levels, public school libraries, special information agency libraries that are publicly funded, such as museum libraries, publicly supported research collections, and the like. Although the libraries of privately owned institutions, such as private academic libraries, libraries of associations, and private collections are overseen by members of the institutions and their elected representatives, some public money, particularly federal money, has gone toward their support through grants of one kind or another; and along with the dollars have come responsibilities to be met. At one time, the amount of public money in support of these privately owned institutions and their libraries was substantial. In recent years, there has been a steady reduction in the amount of public support and these institutions have gone directly to the public for some of that support. Libraries in the for-profit sector are a part of business and industrial research and development programs and many also serve as records management centers for their organizations. Their status and future depend on the extent to which they contribute to the fiscal health of the organization and on the extent to which the internal political structure perceives that contribution. Where federal, state, or local monies support the organization's activity through contractual agreements, here too there is an external political consideration.

Over the past two decades, there have been two major political trends in the planning and funding of services, including publicly supported libraries. One has been the shifting of a number of federally mandated services to the state level and in some cases the shifting of state mandated services to the local level; the other is the taxpayer's revolt against increased levels of taxation.

Because of the economic climate, state revenues have been limited, making it difficult to fund state programs. Add to this the requirement created by the federal government that states fund programs previously funded federally and then compound the states' problems by reducing revenues as a result of a variety of taxpayer initiatives. State government has responded by shifting state mandated programs to the local level where possible and by reducing their support of most remaining programs. Unlike the federal government, state governments are forbidden by law to operate at a deficit.

Fiscal policy is shaped by citizens and elected representatives based on their perception of the environment. Although fiscal policy is to a major extent set at the federal level, taxpayers at the state and local level have been active in proposing and passing legislation which places caps on property taxes, and in some cases actually reduces existing levels of taxation. These taxpayer initiatives stem from a number of causes: concern over rising tax rates, the perception that government is inefficient, costly and wasteful, and frustration by some over support of social programs they do not wish to support. In states where tax caps were passed, the immediate result was a major revenue shortfall.

At the state and local level, the options for fiscal decision making are limited. Taxpayers, although many wish to reduce revenue available to local and state government, do not want those services they use reduced or eliminated. If economic resources in a community are few or declining, the outlook can be decidedly grim. It is easy to allocate resources when there is an abundance, but it becomes increasingly difficult when resources are so limited that basic needs cannot be met. This holds true regardless of the type of government or type of library involved—public, academic, school or special information service.

PLANNING WITH REDUCED RESOURCES

The lines of governance may differ but the problems of carrying out the mission of a library with severely limited resources require that each agency reassess its program and the accompanying costs, and determine how to match the activities and the resources. This activity is variously known as re-evaluation, reassessment, retrenchment, down sizing or right sizing. States and the federal government are reinventing their activities through a number of activities which are intended to simplify process and enhance productivity.

Retrenchment is defined as the situation that exists when the "momentum of expansion has simply outlasted the elastic capacity of the national economy to absorb and pay for it." Retrenchment is necessitated by hard times; that is, when the objectives of an institution must be carried out with reduced resources. Retrenchment is also a way of thinking which can result in a realization that reduced resources provide an opportunity to review programs and to develop new ways to meet objectives. More often, those who face reduced resources do not see the opportunity as much as they see the difficulties.

Financial exigency was defined by Kemerer and Satryb as a crisis in purpose, a crisis in authority and, most important, a crisis in spirit.[1] They indicated that studies of an institution's financial condition provide relative definitions of stress caused by the need to cut back. In the case of the academic library, colleges and universities have been facing difficult times for more than two decades. After years of rapid growth in enrollment, the number of students of college age has leveled off and in some instances has decreased. There has been a shift from full- to part-time attendance in many institutions. The physical plant which grew rapidly in earlier years is now in need of considerable general maintenance. During the post-World War II era, education was viewed as a public good that should be generously supported. In the past decades, beginning with the activism of students in the 1960s public willingness to support higher education lessened as other priorities came to the fore. Decreased support of higher education is due in part to reduced revenues and in part to a lessening of interest on the part of the public. There is little expectation that as the economy grows and tax revenues increase, support of higher education will return to earlier levels.

New methods of reviewing the organization in order to make it more responsive despite revenue reduction focus on the customer, on serving the individual in a faster and more efficient manner. Organizational structures, policies and practices and other activities which interfere with achieving the objective of serving the customer are reviewed and changed until the customer is served in the best possible way. This complex activity is taking place at every level of government, with the federal government deeply involved in reinventing itself.[2] This same emphasis on the customer and customer needs is demonstrated in the many total quality management activities in business, industry and in the not-for-profit sector.[3]

Libraries, as they work to find ways to serve an ever growing public with reduced resources look both at their internal organizational structure to insure that the structure is geared to efficient service and at their programs to insure that they are doing the right things. In a public library setting, re-evaluation takes the form of a thorough program review. Since its inception in 1980, the Planning Process has provided a procedure for evaluation of library objectives and programs.[4] A number of public libraries, often with the assistance of consultants, have reviewed their operations and identified those activities and services that either serve the fewest people or that are most costly, and have eliminated them. The objective has been to reduce specific activities while maintaining the overall integrity of the service program.

A number of public libraries have developed strategic plans, often in cooperation with their user communities to determine what services they should provide and in what way. Knowing that the trend in public library funding is one of slow growth and in many cases reduction, and that the public library is low on the priority list for funding, library leaders have made the only viable response—to review the library's role, to assess resources and to plan for the future, taking firmly into account the need to be well managed, creative and assertive in a period of severe fiscal restraint.

Similarly, academic institutions, and the academic library as part of the institution, have entered a period of retrenchment, financial exigency, or survival at a reduced institutional standard of living. The academic institution and its library, like the public library, must develop a long-range plan, taking into consideration the expected size and nature of clientele, primarily students in this case, what levels of faculty and resources must be maintained to meet educational objectives, and the assumed level of support over the next few years. Priorities in service are needed to insure that the functions of greatest importance will not only be preserved but will grow and develop to meet present and future needs. The academic library, as it moves into the electronic information era, faces major challenges in determining how to deliver service in both print and electronic modes and how to finance the changes which technology mandates.

Planning for a reduced future budget does not necessarily imply a reduced role. A leaner institution will need to meet user needs in innovative ways and respond to informational and educational demands as rapidly as ever. Over-control through a plan for retrenchment is counter-productive and negates the purpose of financial planning, which is to allocate scarce resources in the most responsive fashion. Too tight a plan stifles creativity and rapid response to changing situations. Too loose a plan hinders achievement of objectives and may lead to an unbalanced budget.

The political environment presents the largest overall structure within which planning for service takes place. So interrelated that it is almost impossible to extricate and review independently is the economic environment. Political decisions are made with the public interest or the interests of specific publics in mind. These decisions are usually decisions of resource allocation. In one sense, the economic environment is a reflection of the political environment, from a slightly different angle.

PLANNING FOR INFORMATION PROVISION

Relating economics and information requires two different approaches. One is concerned with the cost of information as a commodity and the other with the cost of delivering information to appropriate clienteles.

Forrest Horton has called information intangible, amorphous, abstract. If you can't see it, how can you budget for it? He says that information must be treated like any asset or resource. When developing a project, one must consider personnel costs, costs of raw materials, of utilities, of physical plant, and the cost of information. To an extent, the cost of information is determined by who packages it, how it is packaged and how it is accessed. Cost is also determined by the expense of locating appropriate information as well as the initial costs of creating it and indexing it. As one puts a cost value on information, the idea that somehow information floats about freely is disabused. Information cost becomes visible. "Being visible, it is a subject of scrutiny and the efforts of the planner are more closely and carefully directed to collect only that information held to be absolutely necessary."[5]

Continuing with the concept of information as commodity, Robert Landau, of The Science Information Association, characterized information as having value like labor, capital and goods; as having measurable characteristics, and inputs that can be transformed into outputs, thus achieving organizational goals. It can be capitalized and spent, and can be treated as other expenses, subject to cost accounting and control. Information is not free and if it is made freely available to a clientele, it is because someone is subsidizing that availability.[6]

In addition to its value as a commodity, information is considered to be a public good in the economic sense. The concept of providing a public good, as stated by Adam Smith, is that "the duty of establishing and maintaining highly beneficial public institutions and public works which are of such a nature that the profit they could earn would ever repay the expense to any individual or small number of individuals to provide them [is the duty of government]. . . . It cannot be expected that the funds for these services would be supplied in adequate quantities [by private means]."[7] Public goods include defense, law and order, and support of the sovereign government. The definition also covers public works, those services that the private sector does not or would not provide because the benefit is widespread and costly. These include roads, schools, colleges and libraries. A public good is not exclusive but is available to and consumable by all citizens in equal amounts. No one can be excluded from using it because of failure to pay for it voluntarily. While the motivation of the private sector is to meet goals, the motivation of the public sector is to consider the welfare of its citizens. Taxes are the price paid for public goods.

Consumers demand both private and public goods and any one individual's demand may differ from another's. As the political system is built on majority rule, large groups, still minorities, may be paying for public goods they do not want and which they object to subsidizing. A special police force to combat crime may be seen as a necessary public good by one group of taxpayers and as unduly repressive by others. Public expenditures of money or education come under fire as some taxpayers question the need for programs which are seen as a necessity by others. Library service is a public good that historically has caused little controversy, perhaps because the funding for library service has been such a small percentage of overall expenditures. As the resources available to provide public goods become increasingly scarce, however, all programs come under close scrutiny and it is those with the largest and most vocal bodies of supporters that seem to survive best. Library service is approved in principle by most citizens and their representatives, but funding that principle is often more difficult. Library service is seen as an asset, pleasant to have, but not basic to the health and survival of the community it serves.

Further attacks on the library as a public good have come from the for-profit sector. There the argument is that information is expensive to develop, has value as a commodity, and therefore should be sold in the marketplace. It has been suggested by some that the library that provides information free (because of subsidy) is in conflict with the free enterprise system and the open market. As we move to a networked information society, this argument increases in intensity. What are we as informed citizens entitled to receive at no additional cost and for what should we pay additional dollars?

Projections of what will occur in the economics of information delivery are dependent upon a number of factors. First of these is the role of policy at national, state, regional and local levels. With the development of information networks and the public realization that information is the basic commodity for all of our activities, development of a national information policy is a high national priority. Questions of who owns the networks, who uses the networks, and the role of the public interest in network development and the resulting access to information are difficult but necessary questions to answer.

Policy is an output of political systems and a product of historical, environmental, economic and cultural forces. Although decision-makers at state and local levels are dependent on the economic forces within their jurisdictions and have limited control over those forces, there are some trends which can help to some extent in anticipating future actions. It appears that we are in a period of rapid change as we move from an era of industrial giants that did things the old way, to an era of the virtual corporation where flexibility and rapid response to market needs are the norm. Old technologies are being replaced by ever newer and faster means of production. Economic growth has been slow, due in part to these major changes. Many of the advances in social services and benefits to citizens have receded as funds to support programs are no longer available. Library service was one of the last programs to benefit from the Great Society and to some degree it is among the more vulnerable services in periods of restrained growth. Dollars for library service are and will continue to be hard to find.

Information as a commodity, however, continues to grow in volume and its production to increase in price. The private sector continues to develop information access programs, tools, and research capabilities for which it charges at the market rate. Subsidized information services will be increasingly hard-pressed to function in competition with the for-profit services. One result has been the availability of fee-based services in publicly supported information institutions. Because this practice collides with the idea that information in a democratic society must be free (i.e., supported through taxation and available to all citizens), it has created considerable controversy. Discussion continues on the issue of what should be free and what should be subject to a fee.

GOVERNMENTAL STRUCTURE IN PLANNING

A library/information agency can be part of any type of organization. The kind of governance structure within which a library operates determines its sources of funding and to whom it is accountable. The three main types of governance structures are: for-profit, nonprofit, and government. Libraries in business environments exist to serve the profit-making function and their resources are used to support product research, design of promotional activities, provision of market information, improvement of internal management and similar tasks. In a for-profit situation, the library is supported to the extent that management perceives its role in increasing profits. When a company is successful and when that success can be in part attributed to an efficient information activity, support can increase. When a company is having difficulties in the marketplace or when there appears to be no direct link between information services and success, the library's budget is at risk. The manager of the corporate information service is responsible for providing services that meet the needs of research staff, administration, and support personnel. If the information service is seen as central to the organization, the manager may report directly to a line officer. If it is seen as marginal, the reporting relationship may be to a staff officer. Increasingly, research teams include an information specialist who is charged to obtain data relevant to the research project and to work closely with the manager of the information center.

The non-profit organization exists to serve a defined clientele and its objective is to benefit the public. Non-profit organizations include such professional associations as the American Association of University Professors and the Modern Language Association of America, and such cultural organizations as theater groups, music associations, museums, and art galleries. They include social agencies, health agencies and hospitals, private academic institutions, and such service agencies as the Girl Scouts or the YMCA. Each is governed by a board elected by and from its membership, membership being defined as dues-paying members or by some other specifically stated criteria. The executive officer selected by the board carries out policy and is responsible for the operation of the agency. Income derives from dues, fees for service, and grants from individuals, foundations, or the government. The objective is to meet the organization's objectives while staying within budget. The for-profits exist to make a profit, the non-profits exist to improve society.

In the absence of a for-profit measure, there is no single satisfactory way to determine whether a non-profit organization and its library are meeting stated objectives. Accountability and assessment measures which measure the extent to which objectives have been met are becoming standard tools in higher education. While accountability measures measure what the organization has accomplished: the number of programs presented, the number of students graduated, etc., assessment measures look at what the student has learned, how the environment has been improved, etc. Such measures are currently most evident in educational institutions and have not been widely used in other environments. For those who do not use some form of the above measures, there is a tendency on the part of the public to assume that the non-profit organization is poorly managed because it does not produce a tangible product, but rather performs a service which may be difficult to quantify. While social cost and benefit are more important than exact quantification, it is admittedly true that some less than able managers use this as a rationale for sloppy management.

The emphasis in non-profit agencies is on the client rather than on the product. Libraries that are part of non-profit agencies exist to serve the needs of the members of their organizations. The private academic library exists to support the educational program, those individuals who carry it out (faculty, staff) and those who benefit from it (students). The profit motive is not part of the objective. While in the case of the for-profits the number of clients is critical to success, the non-profits are less affected by the size of the market. To an extent, a non-profit agency lives on a fixed annual income, knowing at the beginning how much money will be available for the ensuing year. The unit costs will decrease if the number of clients increases, but income does not increase as the number of clients increases. A further factor influencing non-profit organizations is that they tend to be dominated by professionals—by educators, librarians, health care providers and similar individuals. They hold dual allegiances—to their profession and its organization as well as to the institution for which they work. If they are managers, this may be a secondary activity; they are often full-time professionals and part-time managers. Promotion tends to be based on professional competence rather than on managerial skill. Professional education tends to be thin on the teaching of managerial skills; library and information science educational programs rarely require more than one or two courses in management.

Non-profit organizations tend to be political, and the extent to which the non-profit organization responds to political factors is often determined by the extent to which it is dependent on public funding. The library or other agency dependent upon tax monies—the public academic institution, the public school, public library and government agencies, with their libraries and information services—is directly dependent upon the budgets passed by elected officials. These agencies, as part of the government structure, are directly dependent upon the votes of the legislature, city council, or other elected body for their funding. A board of trustees or other body may make policy for the institution and its library, or it and the library may be a department of the government agency which funds it and to which it is directly responsible. This structure determines the process for financial planning.

Each library has an indication of its primary clientele; that clientele is determined to a large extent by the source of the library's funding. The primary clientele of the for-profit library is those individuals—employees of the business—who require specific types of information to perform their jobs. Only employees or others who are given special permission are permitted to use the library resources. The clienteles of a not-for-profit library vary according to the governing body and the limitations it sets. A museum library may be used by the members of the funding association and by those whose information needs meet the specifications set forth by the association. A private academic library has as its primary clientele the students, faculty and staff of the academic institution. Libraries supported by tax monies are available to those paying the taxes. The public library is open to all residents of the city, town, or county who pay taxes in support of the community in which the library is located. Public schools and colleges, too, are tax-supported. Their primary clientele consists of the enrolled students, faculty and staff. As more and more residents return for continuing education and as funds for information resources continue to be difficult to obtain, cooperation between publicly supported schools and the public library is increasing the primary clientele of both groups of libraries. Other publicly supported libraries may have restricted clienteles determined by their specific purpose. Information in for-profit agencies may well be restricted because it is produced for internal use and deals with product information necessary to a particular business. Information in government-supported information agencies may be restricted if it relates to national security, personnel records, or other sensitive data.

LIBRARY INTERRELATIONS AND NETWORKS

The clientele served, the source of funds, and the policies of the governing body may also determine the extent to which a library will interact with other information resource agencies, and the extent to which it will join in some sort of resource-sharing activity. The major resource-sharing efforts have occurred largely for two reasons—too many newly published materials for any one library to purchase and too little money available to obtain those materials. There has also been a major shift on the part of many libraries from a belief that ownership of materials is essential, to the recognition that access to information wherever it may be provides information seekers with a wider range of resources. Given the exponential increase in published information, it is no longer possible or even desirable for any one information agency to own or control all of the information its clientele may need.

Early sharing efforts tended to be limited to a single purpose or to a defined region and were closely tied to the needs and interests of specific libraries or types of libraries. Shared cataloging through utilities such as OCLC and RLIN has gained acceptance and is now standard practice. Development of systems of public libraries on a statewide basis began in the 1950s and these libraries have four decades and more of experience with cooperative efforts. This trend began largely as a result of the Library Services Act (LSA) in 1965 and its successor, the Library Services and Construction Act (LSCA) of 1961, and is still in force (these are discussed on pages 137–39). This effort has been funded to a large extent by LSCA I and III funds with supplementary state support. It began as a federally initiated activity and the commitment to sharing among public libraries varies among the states. As these basic public library networks became more sophisticated, many included school, academic and special libraries in their sharing. Academic libraries came to resource-sharing later, although cooperation among certain academic and research libraries has been underway for some time.

With the development of research networks among universities and research agencies such as ARPA (Advanced Research Projects

Agency) and DARPA (Defense Advanced Research Projects Agency), which were initially intended to allow researchers at different institutions to work cooperatively on projects, linkages have been built which now are the basis for much more comprehensive networks. While universities were the pioneers in the development of data-sharing networks, the effort has grown to encompass national and international telecommunications organizations. State government agencies, for-profit carriers, the entertainment industry and many more have become players in the development of information highways and networks. Just as we are becoming a global economy, so are we building international information connections. The development of these electronic networks to transmit information is perhaps the single most important development of the decade. Libraries as entry points for users and as holders of vast stores of information are central players.

Several states are developing strategic plans for technology which include networking of resources within the state and connections to resources beyond its boundaries. The emphasis here is on access to information by and for its citizens. For-profit companies see the development of networks as the next great investment opportunity. The federal government's role is one of facilitation of network growth which will address the necessary balance of public and private concerns. While the technology is now available, progress will depend upon agreements on policies and procedures and on the availability of dollars to fund growth.

As different types of libraries and information centers with differing clienteles and governance structures continue to explore cooperation through resource-sharing and networking, problems of funding, of ownership and the rights of primary users will occur. Issues of copyright, intellectual property rights, the right to access to information, and related issues require consideration as part of a national information policy or at least a common set of information understandings. As networks grow and combine to become a true national network with international connections, all libraries are part of this national and to some degree global information structure. The technology has provided us with nearly unlimited means of storing, transmitting and accessing information.

Difficulties in the implementation of many of the new technologies arise from the reactions of individuals and institutions to new ways of doing things. New skills must be mastered. Librarians, who once were thought of as numeric- and machine-phobes, have become talented network users who can pull information from thousands of sources worldwide to meet the needs of a particular individual or task. The large expenses of hardware, software and training have placed a heavy burden on already overstretched library budgets. The technology is available to allow each library, and indeed each citizen, access to a world of information. Our ability to participate in that world is limited by lack of financial resources, the need for training and in some cases a hesitance on the part of decision-makers to embrace the new ways of doing things.

THE ROLE OF PLANNING

We cannot influence the past, only the future, and we do that by our actions today. What actions should be taken to assure that the future of libraries and information services is a good one? This is the role of planning. Planning for the future is based on goals for service and assumptions that there will be growth and changes in services, in clientele, in the nature of information, and in the technology to deliver it.

Future projections of the way in which this environment of libraries will change are hazardous. Most projections are based on an analysis and continuation of present trends, but that presupposes that current variables will not change appreciably. The Delphi method of projection, relying on the best prediction of experts in the field, is also unreliable.

Change is so rapid that the leisure of carefully developed plans that take years to form is no longer practicable. A planning structure is needed that allows for and is adaptable to change and yet meets the goals and objectives essential to information activity. For example, a goal may be set to develop a network of local libraries and then join that network to a larger network. The plans to achieve that goal will require continual modification and change depending upon the development of the technology, the enactment of legislation, the needs of clientele and the availability of money.

Our best oracles predict a continuing accumulation of information and a continuing struggle to organize that accumulation. There will be an increasing centralization of economic and political power and an increasing effort to standardize access to information. One road to this achievement will be through the increasing capacity of technology. To some extent, libraries can assume a better educated and more sophisticated user group. What this projection ignores is that a large group of individuals cannot or does not wish to use this increasingly complex information resource. They include those who lack the skills necessary to take part in a difficult environment: the functionally illiterate, the physically disabled, the individual too poor to take advantage of its access points, and the person who does not have and does not want a computer terminal or other device necessary to obtain information and who rebels at the technology and the increasing sophistication necessary to obtain information.

In long-range planning and projections for the future, the lure of technology is strong but one must be cognizant of the fact that technology does not have all of the answers to information dissemination and that there is a widely diverse population of users who do not have the inclination or ability to avail themselves of automated services. In planning, there must be an awareness of the diverse needs and capacities of various clienteles as well as an awareness of present and potential possibilities offered by technology.

NOTES

1. Frank R. Kemerer and Roland Satryb. *Facing Exigency: Strategies for Educational Administrators.* Lexington, Mass: Lexington, 1977.
2. Daniel Osborne and Ted Gaebler. *Reinventing Government: How the Entrepreneurial Spirit Is Transforming the Public Sector.* Reading, Mass.: Addison-Wesley, 1992.
3. Lawrence A. Sherr and Deborah J. Teeter, eds. *Total Quality Management in Higher Education.* San Francisco: Jossey-Bass, 1991.
4. Vernon E. Palmour, Marcie C. Bellassai and Nancy DeWath. *A Planning Process for Public Libraries.* Chicago: ALA, 1980.
5. Forrest Horton. "Nature, Elements, and Value of Information as a Commodity and as a Resource," *Information Resource Mgmt.* NICE Pre-conference Seminar, Washington, D.C., April 16, 1978, p. 27.
6. Robert Landau. "Manager's Role in Accessing the Impact of Information Technology on Organizational Productivity," *Information Manager.* 2:14 (Spring, 1980).
7. Adam Smith. *Wealth of Nations.* London: Routledge, 1913, Book 5, p. 555.

II.

BUDGETING AS PLANNING

Budgeting is the allocation of scarce resources to meet specified objectives. There is rarely if ever enough land or labor or capital to meet every need, and wants tend to exceed the resources available. The economic system uses resources to produce goods and services. In the private sector, the marketplace and profits determine the amount and availability of resources. In the public sector, government determines the resources available through allocation. Decisions as to how to spend public monies are influenced by economic restraints as well as by noneconomic values, including political, social, and cultural considerations.

Some services can be provided by a public/private allocation of resources, depending upon which can provide them best. An example of this is information searching services, some of which provide in-depth information service to clientele for a fee while others provide subsidized service through a library. Health care and postal services are additional examples of shared public/private resource allocation.

Consumers demand both public and private goods and services. In the private sector, demand is expressed in the items they buy or do not buy. Those things they buy will earn profits which will then be used to develop similar products. In the public sector, demand is expressed through political action: voting and pressure on elected officials to allocate resources to those programs and services which are of greatest interest to the citizenry.

In each case, the majority or the most powerful prevail and in each case substantial minorities may find their wants unaddressed. A less popular brand of soap will not survive in the marketplace despite the loyalty of a small group of buyers. Similarly, a government-funded program that may be admirable but that is not supported by a large segment of the public will not survive for long. The result is that we each get some but not all of the things we want, and receive a number of things we don't want.

When making decisions in the public sector, it is necessary to relate expenditures to taxes. Like any other agency that is supported by government allocations, the library is susceptible to political action—either directly, if there is a vote on a purely library issue, or indirectly when the amount of funding is determined and allocated among agencies. At the federal level, revenues can be adjusted to meet the budget but at other levels of government the budget is adjusted to meet the revenue available. If revenues are down, priority decisions on funding will be made and it is here that much of the political action and negotiation takes place.

THE PLANNING FUNCTION

In recent decades, as management has become increasingly professionalized, there has been a growing emphasis on long-range planning and on strategic planning. The development of long-term goals and of priorities among these goals provides an outline and a guide for the activities of an organization and presupposes that there has been an analysis of the needs of the organization and its client groups. Long-range planning also assumes a high degree of continuity in the organization and in its purposes. People may change, the level of resources in support of goals and objectives may vary, but the fundamental purposes do not change. A library may have a new chief executive, staff may be realigned, the budget may be cut, and certain programs dropped, but the library's fundamental purpose of providing access to information remains the same.

Financial planning, as we have said, is the allocation of resources to achieve certain objectives. It is a combination of the activities needed to outline the future development of an institution or service and the activities needed to place a dollar figure on that plan. In other words, budgeting and planning are, or should be, parallel activities. The budget should be seen as a plan with dollar figures attached.

Essential to the planning function is evaluation, which is an integral part of the budget process. Resources must be managed consistently and systematically in order to use them efficiently. The basic resources are capital, crucial physical assets, times, and knowledge. Each of these and their use must be planned for over time and with consistent application of rules. This does not mean that an agency should be tied to earlier ways of doing things, but rather that the use of resources should follow guidelines. Those guidelines, so far as possible, should respond to planned change as the situation requires. Erratic, unreviewed decisions can cause as much difficulty as the absence of decisions.

Because of the close relationship between service planning and financial planning, budget-makers should be familiar with the planning process. An overview of the process is provided in the remainder of this chapter, leading to a planning-budgeting cycle. Types of budgets are introduced, with attention to the increasing emphasis on the goal-setting and evaluation components which are increasingly evident in the budget process.

PLANNING IN THE NON-PROFIT SECTOR

Long-range planning and budgeting may be more difficult to accomplish in the non-profit sector than in for-profit operations, since determination of the resources available is subject to the pleasure of governing boards and/or political bodies and not just to the marketplace. Resources may not be dependent on the volume of business but on the priority of the objective to be carried out. If there are differing views of what the priorities should be, long-range planning is particularly difficult. If the governing board is weak or if there are political factions of nearly equal strength, the direction of the organization may be in doubt. Another potential problem can occur if the organization is slow to change and adopt new directions in response to the needs of its clientele. In any of these circumstances a long-range plan that does not affirm the status quo may not be accepted.

Planning for service on a long-range basis is something that government consultants have advocated for some time, an indication of the gradual professionalization of government agencies. In recent years, nearly all organizations which rely upon tax dollars have instituted a planning process. In some cases these processes are limited to a single unit, but it is more likely that an overall planning process will encompass a number of governmental units, each of which will respond to a common process while reflecting the individuality of the unit. The influence on planning of elected officials, of employees and of public interests varies. It is often assumed that the mayors of cities have considerable influence over planning and expenditure, but this is not necessarily so. It was found in a study of expenditure and income patterns of thirty U.S. cities over a seventeen-year period that in those expenditure classifications covering major components of the municipal work force (fire, police), the workers' organizations and certain community groups were most influential. In those areas of public good (libraries, parks and hospitals), the benefits of which are widely shared and which do not have large employee support groups, the mayor often has more decision-making power. The areas of planning which are of less immediate and direct influence on economic interests are left to the mayor. The voters and interest groups in the city pursue their objectives and the chief officer can deal with what is left over, although he or she can plan only in accordance with and in response to the established groups and known interests. The successful mayor or other elected official is the one who doesn't rock the boat too much, practices a form of incrementalism, and is responsive to the wishes of various interest groups.

Studies have been conducted to determine the extent to which informal influence—the networks and interest groups that abound in and across organizations—affects decisions about priorities, and funding. Prior to the establishment of Public Action Groups (PACs) it was found that few if any of the groups were considered important determinants in the budget decision process, despite efforts and expenditures by those groups to insure that their profession or interest be influential. In recent years, PACs have wielded increasing power in influencing the success or failure of legislation and the funding which accompanies it. They provide contributions to legislators who support their cause or point of view.[1] While much of the news made by PACs is at the national level, similar groups are attentive to legislation and funding issues at the state and local levels.

FUNCTIONS OF THE BUDGET IN PLANNING

As a planning and decision-making device, the budget has a number of functions. The budget is a detailed plan of action. It is related to the general economic health of the community that supports it. It is an assessment of revenues that can be realistically anticipated. Library budgets are closely tied to the economic environment, close attention to which is one of the best ways to predict anticipated revenue. Not only does budget planning cost out objectives; it also serves as a means of identifying resources.

The extent to which the budget is linked to performance evaluation will determine its value as a motivational tool. Some managers see the budget as a contractual agreement between the funder and the individual(s) responsible for carrying out a program, with accomplishments related directly to merit increases. This leads to the use of the budget as a means of evaluating whether or to what extent stated objectives have been met. As with any planning process, the budget process informs those who put the document together of the interrelationship of programs and the way in which each is dependent upon another. As budgeting is the allocation of scarce resources among competing programs, the final document reflects the interrelationships of the programs and decisions.

The budget serves additional functions which have been discussed by Wildavsky at some length.[2] He describes the budget as a political act, in that resources are requested from a funding body. It is a plan of work, as the next year's activities are outlined in terms of the costs of achieving stated objectives. The budget is a prediction of what the staff wishes to accomplish. It can enlighten and it can hide objectives, depending upon the political climate, personal interest, and the skill of the planner. It is a mechanism of control, since the level of overall funding and the amount of funding per program will determine to a large extent the level of activity permitted.

The budget is much more than a document describing programs through the listing of items of expenditure. It is a series of conscious or implied goals with price tags; it is a contract to perform certain functions for a certain fee; and it is mutual agreement. It is a statement of the library's expectations: what must be done and what resources are necessary to do it. Once accepted by the funding body, the budget is a precedent. New programs or positions added to the budget have a good chance of continuing. In sum, the budget is a planning tool that is basically a political document.

LONG-RANGE PLANNING

The role of planning is to project where the library should be in one, three, five or more years, and what must be done to reach the projected level of service. The projection is based on what is needed to achieve desired goals. The budget is the costing out of that plan for the future. Some planners recommend developing a three- to five-year budget projection with each annual budget, looking forward to the longer-range goal. In special instances, a project budget that lasts for more or less than a year is appropriate. Budgeting and planning are entwined throughout the planning process, although it is toward the end of the planning process that the budgeting aspect becomes more readily apparent.

Planning and decision-making involve many separate but inter-related choices and require many different types of expertise. Each expert is likely to have differing views of what the appropriate decisions should be. The accountant, the city budget officer, the university budget officer, faculty committees, and the information specialist will perceive needs differently. Not only does their exper-tise vary; so do their objectivity and their levels of planning ability. To bring these views together, it is necessary to know what resources are available, what the objectives of the library are, and what the need for library services may be.

> Budgets and plans embody the chief comprehensive decisions made by individuals and organizations. To prepare them requires an extremely broad perspective involving an awareness of all feasible alternative actions and of all available resources. The decision-maker's goal is to make the best possible match between the two. Underlying such decisions is a weighing of alternative possibilities and a mental shifting of resources from one potential use to another and an estimation of the effect. This process cannot feasibly be replaced by a series of individual decisions. Accordingly, the conceptual basis for comprehensive decisions is different from that employed to make single decisions, even though both pursue the same goal—the opti-mum use of resources.[3]

THE DECISION-MAKING PROCESS

A decision is a choice among alternatives from which one selects a future course of action. The decision process consists of six steps:

- gathering of information and preliminary problem review
- review of goals and objectives on which the decision rests

- development of a model of the situation under consideration based on the elements and relationships involved
- listing of alternatives
- evaluation of alternatives
- selection of the most feasible alternative.

Objectives are based on policies and are part of a plan. In a not-for-profit situation, decisions relate to the way in which resources are to be used to achieve objectives. Those resources are not owned by the library but belong to the city, the trustees of the university, the state, an association or other group.

From the planning process and the review of various goals and objectives emerge decisions on the most appropriate means of meeting goals and objectives. Usually there are alternative means of achieving an objective and these are evaluated to determine the most appropriate course of action. Although goal-setting and decision-making are groups of activities requiring data analysis, discussion, and negotiation, the final decisions should be centralized. If there is essential agreement, this is not a problem. When there is disagreement, however, one person (or group) must take responsibility.

PRIORITY SETTING

Within an educational institution, a company, an association, or a government agency, priorities are set as part of the planning process. Certain activities will be considered of high priority, others of medium priority, and some will be given low priority status. In an educational institution, classroom instruction and faculty salaries may have a high priority. Access to laboratories and laboratory equipment and library service may have a medium priority, while maintenance of physical plant may have a low priority—until something breaks down. Within a company, research or manufacturing may have a high priority. Within a local government structure, police and fire services typically have a high priority while library services have a medium to low priority.

Setting priorities for allocation of resources is an important aspect of long-range planning. Library planners should be aware that the consideration library services receive is determined in large part by the library's placement on the priority list of the larger organization of which it is a part. From a political point of view, the priority level and the resource allocation level of a service will indicate the way in which the service is perceived, the value that is attached to it. A change in priority level or in resource allocation signals a change in power and in the perception of value.

FACTORS GOVERNING BUDGETING/PLANNING DECISIONS

In discussing budgeting for information services, certain definitions and understandings are necessary. We have already noted the difference between the public sector and the private sector as determined by the services each tends to perform and the sources of funding for those functions. The differences between for-profit and not-for-profit agencies have also been discussed. In each of these instances, the emphasis is on the determination of who should perform certain activities, and the consensus is that the public sector's role is to carry out those activities which the private sector cannot or will not undertake.

Public sector activities should be administered at the proper level of government. Library service can best be provided if a large number of clients is to be served. This may imply that a multijurisdictional service is a valid objective.

The rule of thumb in deciding between public and private sector support is that if a service is too comprehensive and promises little return over the short term, it is a job for the public sector. In some areas of public sector operations, such as the postal service, the private sector has found parts of that service economically viable and has developed competing delivery services in certain areas. Likewise in library and information service, a number of information activities have been identified as profit-making and an information industry has emerged to provide value-added information services to a wide range of paying clients.

Terms such as economic growth, economic stability, and equity are often used in the planning, budgeting process. Economic growth is an increase in the real per capita income and is based on the decisions of government, business, and citizens to invest rather than to consume resources. There is often a conflict between growth and humanitarian values. If those holding capital invest it in economic growth it cannot be used for basic research, for education, food, or medical care. There is always a tugging between economic growth to promote future income and spending now to meet a social need. Economic stability is a condition of high employment and constant prices. Inflation, with a resultant loss in purchasing power, is economically and politically dangerous. The federal government is in a position to make adjustments that could ease the problem when inflation threatens to grow too rapidly, but economists are not always in agreement on the appropriate measures. Equity, in the context used here, is the fair sharing of economic burdens.

A public good—and library service in the public sector is defined as a public good—is an activity that in some way enhances our way of life. Its benefits do not stop at political boundaries and are difficult to measure. Education is a public good in that it benefits all citizens and its effects are far-reaching. Although of general benefit, public education is supported by taxes from specific jurisdictions, supplemented by state and federal aid. Education, like other public goods available to all people, would not be a profit-making venture and therefore is publicly supported. Recently, private sector groups and public schools in some urban areas have experimented with having private sector groups assume the management of selected public schools. Often these are special needs schools within a larger system and the private sector is expected to provide specialized programs and equipment to support the teaching/learning process. It is too early to predict how the public/private relationships in public education will develop or what the eventual result will be. And, of course, there are areas where the private sector provides education to those willing and able to pay enough to sustain the effort. In education, most groups providing a non-public service do so less with a profit motive in mind than to achieve particular educational goals. Libraries are analogous. They cross all divisions and are found in public agencies, in private non-profit agencies, and in for-profit agencies.

A further identifying factor describing a public good is that the activity performed is in the public interest; it has a high social benefit over a long period. Increasingly, public good ventures are being funded by a mix of local, state, and federal funds. Local jurisdictions are often unwilling to fund a service that serves the general good rather than a local need. The sharing of cost with other levels of government is an important step in overcoming this reluctance.

There is a feeling among some groups that the urban areas pay the taxes that support public goods and that the suburban and rural areas get a free ride. Studies of spillover in services tend to discount this, since those who use urban resources such as libraries, museums, and hospitals also do their shopping in urban areas and pay sales taxes. Spillover of services is to an extent related to the distance between potential users and services. When funding of public goods is assumed by county and state agencies, and this is becoming common in many areas, more local concerns about who pays and who receives become moot.

Library service has also been called an "option value":

> . . . library service has important option attributes that might be thought of as the demand not to be disappointed should you decide to purchase the service. . . . Options have a type of public good characteristic because more than one individual can have the benefits of the option at the same time. Given reasonable assumptions about patterns of libraries and hospitals, it is possible to provide options at a lower cost per person as the number of option purchases increase.[4]

Because it is cheaper for all concerned to purchase options in a public service and to have it freely available than to purchase private options, libraries are subsidized.

THE OUTDATED INCREMENTAL APPROACH

In budgeting for services, a common procedure is to adopt an incremental approach. Using this method, the previous year's services are taken as a base and a small incremental increase is automatically added. This can be done without planning or any review of goals. There is no need to collect supporting information since there is no relationship between what you get and what you accomplished. When an external funding body takes the incremental approach, it is an indication that little or no long-range planning has taken place at that level and that there is little or no understanding of the library's purpose or objectives. The main objective of the funding body is to continue the status quo as far as possible by supporting existing programs and going along with what has been done in the past. In this way, no one gets too upset at the way in which funds are allocated.

Equally, when funds are very limited, a percentage decrease is assigned to all or most agencies. Everyone gets something. Those with greater clout get a little more. The funding agency has not done anything very different from the previous year and therefore can, if questioned, point to precedent. When making funding decisions in particularly difficult times, salaries tend to be the first priority, with operating expenses, supplies, materials, equipment and maintenance following. Not only does incrementalism maintain the status quo; it also keeps employees safe politically and hides the fact that some of them may lack the necessary expertise to function in the changing environment.

> The simplistic decision criteria that are used by many state and local budget makers may help them cope with the complexities of political-economic issues and fractured institutions, but they provide little encouragement to those who would use the budget process as the vehicle for program planning.[5]

> As a conservative bulwark, the budget may permit legislative bodies, administrators, and private interests to tolerate competition for change because no radical change is likely to survive the funding process.[6]

The budget, as Wildavsky indicated, can be a means of control. The amount of money a library receives will to a considerable extent determine what it will be able to do. When planners began looking at the budget process as an integral part of the planning activity, they found that under the incremental approach planning was not relevant and that to change the planning/budgeting process it was necessary to go against the prevailing political managerial climate—in effect, to be reformers. These reform activities have been successful to such a degree that relatively few individuals involved in the budget process continue to rely on an incremental approach.

Implicit in the planning and budgeting process is the need to account for the way in which monies are spent. In the incrementalism environment, a brief indication of monies spent per item may have been all that was required. In the planning/budgeting modes which are program- or performance-oriented, a more sophisticated form of evaluation is necessary. The people and agencies who fund libraries have the right, often the legal right, to know how their money was spent and what they got for it. Accounting methods, evaluation programs and reporting activities can and should serve this purpose.

EARLY STEPS IN THE BUDGETING PROCESS

The first step in budgeting is planning, and the first step in planning is data gathering. Those who conduct the planning activity should be representative of each important area of the library's operation and of service groups. They should include representatives of library administration, department heads, professional staff, senior nonprofessional staff, and representatives of the library's user groups. These latter might be public library patrons, researchers, students, or some combination. The planning committee, small enough to be functional but large enough to be representative, is an important element in the planning process, both because of the different viewpoints represented and because of the importance of including participation in the decision-making process. From a functional standpoint, one or two committee members may do most of the data collection and present the results to the full committee for review.

Although representation of the views of the various groups involved in information service is most desirable in planning, there are a number of other ways to go about the task. In some organizations, an autocratic method of planning is pursued. Top management determines goals and objectives, sets priorities and prepares operating budgets. The accomplished fact is then delivered to those who are charged with implementation. A slightly more democratic process allows ideas and suggestions from those responsible for implementation. Neither of these is as effective has having a well-chosen planning group.

Information for planning includes a scan of the environment within which library service is provided, both externally and internally. It is important to understand the social, economic, educational, demographic and technological trends which will affect kinds of library service and the levels of funding over the next several years. Although the identification of trends may be no more than very educated guessing, it does bring together information available from many sources which can be useful in setting a course. In addition to collecting data which are useful in identifying trends, up-to-date data about existing clientele and issues are also necessary. Many libraries have conducted community analyses which detail the population served and its characteristics, such as age, education, and ethnic background. The community as a whole is described in the analysis in terms of its setting (urban, suburban, rural, its cultural heritage, its economic bases, and its standard of living). Combining the environmental scan and the library's community analysis with the long-range plans and projections of regional planning agencies and other groups involved in planning provides a good basis for determining the potential clientele of the library and the community to be served, as well as identifying the larger information and economic environments within which each library operates.

Internally, the library's resources need to be identified—the book stock, periodicals, recordings, access to electronic information resources and services, etc.—and the rate of growth of each. How large is the library's staff, what are its duties and how are these duties expected to change in the next year in response to such influences as administrative reorganization, new technological skills to be mastered or an anticipated change in clientele? What services does the library now provide and how are they used in the community served? Trends can be identified by reviewing statistics. Also, what other collections, electronic connections and information agencies exist in the community and how are they used by the library?

At some point, early rather than late, a formal statement of library purposes is needed. This mission statement can grow out of professional concerns, can be a statement of expectations of the funding agency, or can result from client expectations and demonstrated need. Ideally, the statement or informal agreement of purpose should identify with and respond to a combination of these.

Although all libraries and information agencies need to analyze their communities in order to identify the clientele served and not served, and in order to develop a comprehensive plan, the public library has been the most active in data collecting and analysis. As academic libraries move more aggressively into the electronic environment and as specialized information agencies continue to be pressured to justify their services, they have shown greater interest in analyzing their clienteles. While the academic library and the specialized information agency may have more restricted clienteles than a public library, they also need to analyze their clientele in order to relate services and resources to client needs and interests. There are many characteristics which are important to identify. For example, the undergraduate student body in the average academic institution could at one time be described as 18–24 years old, full-time, and resident on or near campus. Today, however, more and more students are waiting before they begin study or are returning to school after a number of years away. Approximately forty percent of the student body nationally attends part-time[7] and many part-time students are employed full- or part-time. These students have competing demands on their time and require different types of service support than do students who are pursuing formal education full-time. Student bodies are also increasingly diverse, representing all facets of our social, economic and ethnic environment. This has implications for collection development and service provision. Existing services need to be reexamined to determine if they are appropriate and if so, what percentage of students take advantage of the services. New services or reconfigurations of existing services may be necessary to meet current student needs. A major benefit of moving to an environment in which information is increasingly available electronically is that the part-time student has access to catalogs and other information from sites other than the library. Typically, the academic library maintains good internal data concerning holdings and uses of services. These are important in planning but represent only a portion of the data needed. It is the combining of internal use and program data with community analysis that determines the fit of the two and serves as a basis for planning. The same holds true for all information services. The initial step in planning and budgeting is an analysis of those being served and the extent to which the library's purpose is being met. This latter is determined by the match between clientele and the resources and services performed.

With the increasing emphasis on accountability both in the public and the private sectors, it is important to look at what the library wishes to accomplish in terms of services and to build into the planning process strategies for measuring that accomplishment. The emphasis on inputs (size of collection, size of staff), or outputs (how many titles cataloged, reference questions answered) has given way to an emphasis on outcomes (what did the student learn? how has the information provided to a small business aided that business?). This is much more difficult to measure but its value is that it places measures of success on changes in the environment and the satisfaction of the consumer.

As with the public library and its relationship to regional plans, in those cases where the academic institution, the association, agency or company of which the library is a part has developed a long-range plan, library planners should be familiar with it and be aware of the role that the larger entity sees the library playing. If the library is assigned an inadequate role, then the library planners should seize the opportunity to expand the library role and to integrate the expanded role into the plan. Academic planning groups tend to focus on academic program rather than on support services such as libraries and computing services. It is the task of the library faculty and staff to insure that faculty and administration understand the relationship between academic program decisions and library support.

Once the planning committee has collected the necessary information concerning the library's community and information describing resources and program, and once the committee has a firm grasp of the library's role in the community it is designed to serve, evaluative measures need to be developed. Here there is a mix of outcome measures which determine the extent to which the customer's learning or satisfaction was enhanced by the service and measures which look at the management of the library. To what extent is the library meeting its purpose of providing information service? What is the level of that service and what are the costs? If there are multiple library outlets, is there a difference among them in levels of service, levels of satisfaction, in cost of service? Current services are also evaluated in relation to perceptions of the staff. What areas of the programs do they perceive as weak? What areas are adequately supported and working well? Staff input into program evaluation is important; this is the group that works daily with program and these are the experts in their program's implementation. To measure outcomes, library users need to have the opportunity to assess program quality and their level of learning and satisfaction as a result of their participation. Their perceptions may or may not be based on fact but they carry political weight and must be considered in the planning process.

Comparison with other libraries serving similar clienteles or offering similar programs is also helpful in evaluating the library's performance. If up-to-date standards and/or planning guides relevant to the library's environment are available, these too can be used.

REVIEW OF GOALS AND OBJECTIVES

Once the community information and the current status information are available, it is time to review the goals and objectives of the library to determine whether the library's performance is in accordance with them. If the goals and objectives of the library have not been reviewed for some time or if there are no stated goals and objectives, it is important to develop new ones based on the information accumulated in the earlier planning steps. Goals and objectives are based to a large extent on the perceived needs of the clientele to be served and the need to meet their "customer demands." This is expressed in terms of types of services, resources needed, hours that service is available, and location of service outlets. Goals for types of service—e.g. "expanded reference service"—are addressed to a "service need." A goal for collection development meets a resource need that is service-oriented. In the case of the research library, it is also oriented toward the development of and access to knowledge in the subject area.

Objectives, which are goals broken into more specific terms, follow from the purposes, and should be concretely measurable. For example, the reference collection development goal can be broken into a number of objectives, including the addition of certain major business reference tools, of on-line bibliographic service, of access to the Internet or other information resources and services. The cost of each objective can be determined and the extent to which the objective was met can later be examined. Each goal and objective contributes to the overall purpose of the library's services, which should be planned as an integrated whole.

This process of data gathering, analysis, and goal revision or development is very time-consuming. Necessary data may take time to collect and viable goals and objectives require discussion and negotiation among the committee members. Sometimes there is no time for careful planning and decisions must be implemented quickly. If fairly up-to-date goals and objectives are in place, rapid planning/decision-making is made easier. In this shortened planning mode, the library manager and department heads are usually the persons involved. To the extent possible, this group should restrict its activities to tactical rather than long-range planning. Short-term solutions that do not damage the overall program may have to be made on short notice, but short-term planning should not be adopted as a way of making basic changes.

When rapid planning is necessary (and it is no substitution for well developed, long-range planning), some guidelines are needed. Most importantly, set a tight schedule with deadlines. Assign responsibility to one person to monitor the process. If financial cuts are the motivation for the abbreviated planning process, determine in advance the approximate size of the cut. As the process evolves, maintain a record of all decisions made and the rationale for them. Regardless of the time constraints on planning, the procedure should be carefully thought out and all relevant data should be marshalled. Having indicated the need for a thoughtful procedure, it is also important that the person responsible for the activity be able to take advantage of unforeseen opportunities or to respond to a crisis situation. The thoughtful process can serve as a support structure for decisions requiring immediacy.

In an austerity environment, despite reduced resources the planner must maintain a balanced program. Cutting back without reference to an overall plan that insures that the major goals of the library are met can destroy or seriously undermine the organization. It may be necessary to review the goals of the library and revise them in the light of changes in resources, or perhaps to eliminate some activities altogether. However the decisions are made, the budget itself must not only be in balance but must also reflect a balanced approach to organizational goals. To achieve this,

> Librarians and budget officers . . . will have to get into, under, and behind the totals of publishers' invoices and the summary of the payroll. The evidence on which budgets must be built will entail descriptive statistics and a working knowledge of the forces during cost increases. Taking an acquisition budget total and multiplying it by a single cost rise factor won't provide enough information for intelligent budget decisions; it won't reveal what trade-offs are being made, which factors are stable and which uncertain, where future expectations are firm and where soft, what policy alternatives exist and at what cost.[8]

Libraries tend to be conservative institutions. When times are good there is a tendency to do more of what is currently done rather than to rethink what is being done to determine whether it should be done at all. With the front and center role of libraries in the world of the national information infrastructure and the world of digital information, many aspects of the library's organization, staff skills, services and customer expectations are changing. Rethinking of existing objectives and the concurrent development of new objectives to meet present and future needs is a particularly challenging activity when budgets are tight.

TYPES OF BUDGETS

There are two major types of budgets—the operating budget and the capital budget. The operating budget is funded on a year-by-year basis and, as its name implies, is the source of those funds available to carry out the library's program for the year. The capital budget is separate from the operating budget and is not usually developed on an annual basis.

The purpose of the capital budget is to provide a source of funding for major changes or improvements, such as the purchase of land for future growth, the building of a new library, major equipment purchases and the like. Whereas the operating budget is determined annually and its funds are part of annual income expectations, the capital budget is long-term and can be funded from a number of sources depending on the organization of which the library is a part and the laws and regulations that apply.

In a publicly supported library, it may not be possible to maintain a capital budget fund, but in a privately supported agency the practice is quite common. Typically, if the library and its supporting agency have investments, conduct fund drives, or otherwise receive monies outside those planned for the operating budget, they go into the capital fund. In some instances, the capital budget is an accounting of income from various sources rather than an actual budget. When there is sufficient income to fund a major project, then it is spent. In other cases, the capital budget is a carefully planned program of anticipated need, from which an active fund-raising campaign is developed. Universities often have a separate capital budget which is used to fund the university building program. New library buildings and major renovations are incorporated into the overall plan. Special purpose grants awarded the library by government or other agencies are handled separately from either the operating or capital budget.

The question of what constitutes a capital expenditure and what an operating expenditure is often in doubt. Generally, a capital expenditure is something of enduring worth that will not be consumed quickly—a building, new furnishings, a new computer network system. As operating budgets are tightened, library personnel and funding agencies have stretched the definition of capital expenditures to include books and equipment. In one sense of the word these items are capital expenses, since they are not consumed in one year. Such a definition, however, can lead to a dangerous erosion of the capital budget. The capital budget is integral to the planning process. What money is held for or spent on is determined by long-range plans. Further, there should be a clear and planned relation between the capital budget and the operating budget.

The operating budget has a number of variations, four of which— the line-item, program, performance, and zero-base—are the most commonly used or discussed. There are additional variations such as formula-base or lump sum, but these have less impact. Considerable attention will be given to each of these formats later in this volume. The purpose of introducing and briefly describing each of them here is to show how each fits into the planning process.

The traditional budget form is the line-item or object-of-expenditure budget. In this format the expenditures of a service— salaries, books and materials, utilities, etc.—and the amounts projected for each of these are listed. Usually the prior year's budget is used as a guide and expenditures are increased based on an estimate of increased service costs and the rate of inflation. For the incremental approach this is the ideal format, as items can be increased or decreased with little additional information. This is not a planning budget and the library's plan is not obvious from this format. The ingredients of a plan are present but there is no goal or objective listed. It is a bit like describing a loaf of bread by reading off the ingredients rather than by describing the end result.

The line-item budget is easy to formulate because it can be built on the previous year's budget. It is easy to cut since reducing a salary or supply item can be done by the funding agency with no awareness of any program implications. The line-item budget is merely derivative of prior annual figures, it is not a planning document.

In the 1950s the movement toward greater professionalism in the operation of both profit and non-profit agencies had reached the point where planning had gained stature and tools for planning were developed. One such planning tool is the program budget. A program budget begins with the identification of long-range goals for the library, and breaks those goals down into yearly components. The budget is then designed around programs—circulation services, reference services, children's services, and so on. Another formulation is reader's services, technical services, computer network services and maintenance support. For each program, a detailed line-item budget is prepared. This budget emphasizes the tasks to be performed in the library and the cost of each.

The initial development of the program budget is time-consuming, for it is necessary to collect information in formats different from those of the line-item budget. Personnel costs for each program are calculated on the basis of time actually spent on a given task. Each of the traditional line items is split up and costs are assigned to programs.

The program budget is a true planning tool. It requires the development of goals and objectives and an understanding of library services. It is more difficult to cut than the line-item budget because the budget cutters have to deal with programs and can see the implications of their proposed economies. The program budget also informs the funding agency of what the library is doing. Many libraries have moved to this kind of budget in recent years, partly because it is an integral part of the institution's planning process and partly because it serves as a means of providing information about the library's programs. In most agencies, a standard format for budget presentation is required, either by institutional or government authorities. If that format is line-item, many libraries have developed two budget presentations: one in the required form and the second as a planning and informational document.

A third budgeting format, the Planning Program Budgeting System (PPBS) is an extension and refinement of the program budgeting system. In this format each program's existence and the manner in which it is to be implemented must be justified. PPBS also includes a plan for continuous feedback and evaluation so that managers know on a continuous basis the extent to which the library is meeting its objectives. As these objectives are based on the development of output measures—e.g., number of books circulated, number of reference questions answered—and since in a service environment such output measures do not provide a full picture of program effectiveness, the performance budget has not been widely adopted. As the emphasis by local and state government and accrediting agencies is shifting to outcome measures which focus on the results or outcomes of providing a good or a service—e.g. what the student has learned, the benefit to a small business from a reference service, the extent to which a specialized information service can show a relationship between its services and an increase in market share, and similar measures—there has been a greater emphasis on justifying programs and expenditures based on measurable change and customer satisfaction. It is a logical step from this to planning/budgeting systems which focus on the customer and customer satisfaction.

During the 1970s, zero-base budgeting received attention at the national level and as a planning tool was quite helpful. As a budgeting tool its usefulness has been limited. Zero-base budgeting uses many of the techniques common to the other forms of budgeting. The initial step in zero-base planning is to ask whether a particular program is essential and if so to justify its continuation. If this can be done, the next step is to develop a continuum of support for the program ranging from the least possible amount of funding to the ideal funding situation. Each program is developed in this fashion and then the programs are placed in priority order. Funding decisions are then based on the programs' priority positions and the acceptable or possible level of funding of each. This is a complex process that takes time and requires trained personnel to assist in its development. It carries the planning process further than other budgeting formats, in that priorities are agreed upon both for programs to be funded and for levels of support.

Other budgeting formats tend to reflect incrementalism and line-item formats rather than planning input. Formula budgeting is a mechanical activity that is used by some state agencies to determine levels of support for its publicly supported academic libraries. Guidelines for fund allocations are based on such factors as number of students, programs of study and similar quantifiable factors. The library allocation is then ascertained and funds released to the university. A budget is then developed to comply with the resources available.

The most primitive form of budget is the lump sum budget. A library is given a sum of money and told to provide library service. The library then has to develop a budget in conformity with the resources available. In many organizations, the planning process is followed, a plan is developed and a budget set up. The funding agency, operating on the basis of revenues available and the principle of incrementalism, then provides a lump sum to the library. Although there appears to be a mismatch between the planning and funding activities at the end of the budget process, the planning process is still important; it may need to be modified to conform to the money available, but the plan must be present. Thus even in this most elementary form of budgeting, a component of planning is either present or implied.

BUDGET APPROVAL CYCLE

In its broadest outline, the budget cycle can be divided into four parts: preparation and submission, approval by legislature or other administrative body, execution, and audit. Each of these steps involves specific procedures, and formalized models for carrying them out have been developed. Budget preparation begins with the development of goals and objectives. Next comes the preparation of a forecast, which is a general statement of costs. The budget cycle is a year-long activity that begins with planning and does not end until the funds have been spent and accounted for.

The budget year may not coincide with the calendar year. The federal government's budget year, for example, begins on October 1; many academic institutions have budget years that begin July 1 or September 1, while state and local governments may have still different dates for the beginning of their budget years. At whatever time the budget year begins, the planner develops a budget calendar showing dates by which certain activities are to be completed. Those dates should meet any internal deadlines and requirements for completion of tasks at other levels of the planning process, and be in compliance with whatever regulations may exist.

In this cycle, it is assumed that planning has taken place, that goals and objectives are in place, that the budget planning document has been prepared in general outline, and that necessary information for coding and analysis is available. The budget director prepares estimate forms to be used for each department. The forms provide a consistent means of reporting requests for support. Upon return of the forms, the budget director consolidates data and prepares an overall budget estimate. Once this has been done, a schedule of departmental hearings is set up so that each supervisor can discuss budget estimates, justify costs, and present the case for funding his or her department at a certain level. The budget is then modified in response to the information gathered at the hearings and the revised budget is submitted to the library director, who then submits it to the next higher authority.

In the case of the public library, the budget might be submitted to a board of trustees; in the academic library it would go to the fiscal officer of the institution; and in other non-profit agencies to whatever is the appropriate governing body. In the for-profit environment, it would go to the organization's business officer or similar individual. If the governing body is different from the funding body, as in the case of the public library board of trustees, the governing body reviews the budget before sending it on to the funding body. That body will usually conduct a hearing at which representatives of the library board and the director have an opportunity to discuss the total library budget as part of the larger budget of the government, university, or association. For those libraries whose funding comes from the tax base, from contributions, or membership fees, a public hearing permits members and citizens to question budget items, to support or object to the library's program, and generally to exercise their democratic privileges. After the open hearings, the budget is reviewed again and final figures are determined, dependent in the case of non-profit agencies upon anticipated revenue.

This process permits the library to present its program and to request funding for its support. The hearings are an opportunity for library representatives to present their program priorities and needs to a larger audience. It is important to know the individuals who are responsible for the funding decisions and to be aware of the ways in which they operate. In preparing for hearings, a well thought-out presentation is most important. Although the representatives of the funding agency have received the budget proposal, they may not have had time to review it, or if they have, they may find a brief refresher helpful. The presentation by the library representatives should be a brief overview of goals and objectives with special emphasis on priority objectives for the year under consideration. Any new programs and possible program areas should be mentioned so that there are no surprises. Funding groups need as much information as they can get about the status of a program and what is needed to fund it. Judicious use of statistical data and of evaluative measures of past performance is helpful in explaining successes or reasons for less than successful performance. Often, members of the hearing committee are expert in a particular area of the budget, such as personnel, and will ask specific questions about that aspect. Library representatives must be prepared to respond to specific questions promptly and accurately.

Hearings are partly informational, partly political, and only in small part actually financial. It is unwise to attempt to short-circuit the process by suggesting informal deals or resorting to power plays. The rather lengthy process should be played out and played straight, or as straight as possible. In the best of worlds, funding is provided in response to program needs and in accordance with the budget. In reality, the allocation will probably be an incremental percentage increase or decrease related to the estimated state of revenues for the next year. If the amount received is less than what was requested, the library's budget officer will need to review the budget request and reduce it to conform to anticipated revenue.

Throughout the year regular reports are prepared, thus maintaining a record of expenditures for the use of planners and funders. A year-end report provides a summary of the way in which funds have been spent and should also include a statement of the extent to which goals and objectives have been met. An audit of records should take place on a regular basis, not necessarily annually, and should be performed by an outside auditor. This insures that appropriate accounting procedures are being followed and that there is compliance with the law.

The planning/budgeting cycle is sometimes called the management control process. As the diagram[9] on page 43 shows, the management cycle is a continuous process, from programming through budgeting, on to operating and accounting, and ending with reporting and analysis before returning again to programming. External information is fed into the process at a number of points and there are links between reporting and analysis and budgeting. Each of these steps recurs in a regular cycle and forms a closed loop.

The budget cycle requires both political and managerial skills, neither of which is emphasized within the brief professional preparation of information specialists. Getting and spending money for libraries is a complex activity and it is often the successful completion of this task that insures the survival and viability of the library and its services.

PLANNING AND BUDGETING IN A NO-GROWTH ENVIRONMENT

In the period from the 1950s to the mid-1970s, growth budgets were common and planners could expect to add programs and positions.

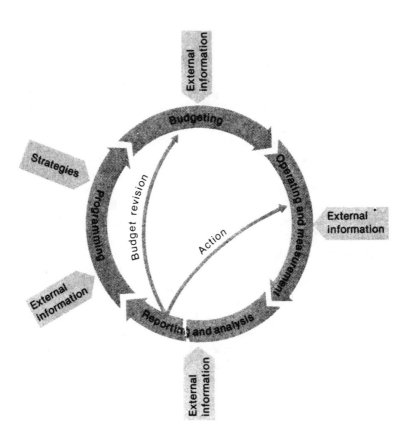

Sequence of Management Control Processes

The past several years have witnessed slow growth, no growth and reduced budgets. The situation has been exacerbated during periods of inflation and by rapid increases in the cost of particular goods and services, such as the annual double-digit increase in the prices of many journals. The no-growth environment is characterized by budget deficits, cuts in services, and increased taxes and tuition and fees, none of which do more than partially meet increased costs. Because publicly funded libraries and the institutions of which they are a part are closely tied to the economy, when business is good, income tends to go up and services to expand. When business is bad and tax collections are down, there is insufficient funding to meet the needs. With the passage in a number of states of caps on the ability to tax, libraries have been particularly hard hit. Many citizens of states in which caps have been approved by the voters have said that they were voting against big government and not against libraries. Although voters have the power to propose and pass amendments, they do not have similar control over the budget allocation process in their communities, but even if they did, they would doubtless fund police, fire, snow removal and similar services before they would fund libraries.

Catch phrases such as "emphasis on academic quality" or "planned development" or "selective development" may be a polite way of masking a steady-state or no-growth budget. Academic libraries have had decades of dealing with reduced resources. As the pool of traditional college-age individuals declines, fewer full-time students attend college. In providing services, part-time students require as much attention as full-time students but generate less revenue for the institution. As academic institutions look at the steady decline in their budgets, programs are reviewed to determine their centrality to the institution, the quality of the program and the resources needed to continue that program. Institutions participating in regional consortia may be able to share resources. The academic library practices resource-sharing and subject specialization, in part in response to no-growth or declining budgets.

When program is seen as product and student or user is seen as consumer, a marketing situation exists. Carrying this further, the institution, if it wishes to be in a good market position, will offer those programs which are in greatest demand and eliminate those which are least attended. This concept, however, fails to take into consideration the expertise of existing faculty or the research support strengths of library and laboratory resources. And it does not take into account the traditional role of the academic institution to pass on learning to each generation. Dante, Goethe, Dickinson, Shakespeare and Tolstoy may not be cost-effective in the marketplace but they are critical to our cultural heritage.

The institution and its library must plan for tomorrow's diverse student body with its broader range of information needs and demand for an increasing variety of formats in which information is available, and marshal resources in such a way as to make the best use of what is available. Cutting back is one strategy. Additional strategies include prioritizing activities, reviewing service delivery mechanisms and building coalitions with other information agencies. Strategies that will allow us to use available resources in new and better ways to achieve intended goals are imperative.

Whatever planning opportunities a no-growth or declining budget present, there are certain to be immediate and difficult repercussions. When funds for part-time employees are cut, services are eliminated or reduced and people lose their jobs. Reduction in full-time positions is usually achieved through attrition unless the cuts are particularly severe and employees, usually those with the least seniority, have to be let go. When personnel leave and funds are not available to replace them, not only is service reduced but the random elimination of expertise resulting from attrition or "last hired first let go" can unbalance service. The reference staff may be depleted while the circulation services staff remains strong, or unfilled beginning professional positions may require senior staff to perform entry-level functions; conversely, a department may be left with no senior personnel. More typically, it is the clerical and maintenance staff that experiences the greatest turnover, leaving the remaining staff to function in poorly maintained buildings and without adequate support.

Strategic planning is essential for the long term but immediate crises may not wait for long-term solutions. Staff cuts may require the closing of branches partially or completely. This can cause hardship to individuals who live at a distance and who may lose their only convenient access to service. Other budget tactics related to staffing cuts include reallocation of duties, a reduced work week and options for early retirement.

Even more immediate than staff cuts can be the impact of reductions in acquisitions allocations, an impact which is intensified by steeply increased costs of information materials and the need to purchase materials in a variety of formats. Even when the acquisitions budget is increased, it may be that fewer materials can be purchased because of the increase in the cost of journals which exceeds the rate of inflation.

Academic library planners may have added difficulty in planning for collection development if the acquisitions budget is allocated to different departments. Each of these, of course, wishes to guard its resources and resists attempts to modify or reduce its existing budget allocation. Planning cuts in such cases requires agreement by academic departments and the administration, in addition to library planners. In some institutions academic departments are less involved in collection development and library planners have greater freedom to build the overall collection. One potential problem here is that curriculum and collection may not be developing in a coordinated manner.

In the public sector the library budget is often subject to the collective bargaining process. A study of several instances of bargaining showed that in difficult fiscal times, collective bargaining is more closely tied to the budget-making process than in favorable times. The ability to pay is basic to any negotiation.

Among personnel budgeting considerations, the cost of living tends to rise more rapidly than the salaries of employees, particularly in the non-profit area. With a steady state budget, there is little opportunity for internal promotion and merit raises are few, much of the available funds being used to meet cost-of-living increases. Employees may become overqualified for the jobs they are responsible for doing if there is little or no internal upward mobility. Nor, in such cases, is there a monetary reward for a job well done. Staff may become restive but many will continue in their positions for fear of not being able to find another job. Job turnover is reduced significantly during difficult economic times. These personnel factors must be weighed in the planning/budgeting activity.

Also worthy of consideration in this process is the cycle of maintenance of equipment and physical plant. This is often the area cut first in a tight budget situation, in the hope that the building will stay intact for one more year or that the computers will last a little longer. Deferred maintenance and deferred equipment replacement can be more costly in the long run than following a regular schedule. A roof left too long without repair may need to be replaced at much higher cost. Aging computers with insufficient memory may take more staff time to use and therefore be more costly to operate than those that are regularly upgraded.

These concerns about the costliness of no-growth budgets are not meant to imply that such budgets close off all opportunities. A steady state provides an opportunity to review past performance and programs, to make choices and to plan for the best use of resources to meet objectives. Some critics claim that there is duplication in library programs, that services are not efficiently managed, or that there are alternatives to current practices. If this is so, it becomes the responsibility of planners to review the situation and develop a flexible and lean program that gives maximum service for each dollar.

The library as part of a larger institution—government, academic, company or association—while it needs to develop its own strategic plan for a no-growth or downsizing situation, can only do so in accordance with the reduced or realigned goals of the larger entity. A wider understanding of the interdependence of library service and other aspects of an organization is necessary for useful long-range planning.

In summary, the planning process should take into consideration the existing plan and the desirability of continuing past operations. It should consider the rapid rate of change, be aware that plans for the future are made on the basis of past experience and that any plan must be subject to continuous revision. There are trends and cycles in the use of library and information services, but there is never any guarantee that they will recur in the same form. Planning is educated guessing but inexact though it may be, it is always preferable to no plan.

NOTES

1. Richard L. Berke, "Pragmatism Guides Political Gifts, a Study Shows," *New York Times* September 16, 1990, p. 26.
2. Aaron Wildavsky, *The Politics of the Budgetary Process.* New York: Little, 1964.
3. Alfred R. Oxenfeldt, *Cost Benefit Analysis for Decision Making: the Danger of Plain Common Sense.* New York: American Management Association, 1976, p. 30.
4. Thomas Cowing and A. G. Holtman, *The Economics of Local Public Service Consolidation.* Lexington, Mass.: Heath, 1976, p. 95.

5. Ira Sharansky, *The Politics of Taxing and Spending.* Indianapolis: Bobbs-Merrill, 1969, p. 95.
6. *Ibid.*, p. 96.
7. *Chronicle of Higher Education.* 40:20, January 19, 1994, p. A34.
8. David S. P. Hopkins, "Computer Models Employed in University Administration: the Stanford Experience." *Interface* 9:2 part 1, February 1979, p. 18.
9. Robert N. Anthony and Glenn A. Welsch, *Fundamentals of Management Accounting.* Homewood, Ill.: Richard D. Irwin, 1971, p. 303.

III

INTERNAL BUDGET MANAGEMENT

Budget decisions are made by people. Individuals and groups inside and outside an organization influence the amount of money made available and how it is allocated. The interplay among people and the planning and budgeting process—staff, middle-managers, general officers, trustees—must be understood if the process is to be managed properly. Budgeting is a balancing of human factors as well as a balancing of numbers.

Planning and budgeting also require both external and internal collection of data. The external aspects of planning are tied to the politics and policies resulting from the larger environment; the internal aspects of management are tied to the necessity of carrying out policy. The way in which they are carried out is dependent upon the managerial style of the organization, the resources available and the communication among the various internal components.

HUMAN FACTORS IN BUDGET-MAKING

Personnel issues have often been cited as the major area of difficulty in planning for an organization. Although technological change can be projected in terms of equipment, individuals are often unwilling to change at the rate and in the ways planners might wish. People change and interact at their own rate and in ways not necessarily in accordance with the expectations of those planning for the future of the organization. A number of factors influence the behavioral aspects of internal management activities. Most organizations are complex, involving a number of constituencies and departments, allegiances and loyalties, each of which has an impact on overall planning. Planning in an organization that consists of groups with differing interests and agendas is very difficult and often results in fragmentation of programs and objectives.

49

In addition to the formal organizational structure, of equal importance is the informal structure—those ways of doing things and the special communication that individuals devise to accomplish objectives. Just as with the formal structure, the informal can become so entrenched that the structure or environment interferes with the planning process. Personal characteristics and the backgrounds of individuals in the organization also affect planning. Factors such as age, length of service, and level of experience in the present organization and in other organizations will affect the performance of individuals in the process.

ATTITUDES TOWARD CHANGE

As participative systems of planning and budgeting are introduced there is often uncertainty on the part of those involved in the process. It has been remarked that change is the only constant in our current environment. Planning processes focus on change, evaluative processes focus on continuous improvement, and staff have come to the understanding that they must continue to learn how to do their job in order to meet the demands of that job. Traditional planning and budgeting which concentrated authority and decision-making in the few has gradually given way to a more open systems approach. There still remain individuals and organizations that are uncomfortable with change. Some will attempt to ignore changes to the extent possible, others will go along with it or appear to do so and then circumvent it as much as they can.

The environment and budget planning activities are interactive, each dependent upon the other. "A budget is not only a financial plan that sets forth cost and revenue goals for responsibility centers within the firm but also a device for control, co-ordination, communication, performance evaluation and motivation."[1]

Budget development as an outgrowth of goal setting can be either positive or negative. If the goals and objectives that are set are too easily attainable, there is little need to exert effort to meet them, and if they are too grand there is also little need to exert effort, since no one could possibly attain them. Goals should be an attainable challenge. Clarity in planning for goals and in translating those goals into the budget format, and a willingness by management to participate honestly in the process, providing feedback when necessary, appear to be the mixture for success in the internal budget planning cycle. Although decision-making has become increasingly less authoritarian, organizations continue to be dependent upon the willingness of those in charge to share responsibility.

Internally, the budget process is a decision-making process involving a number of people. It has behavioral aspects and political aspects. Any decision has a number of variables that need to be dealt with and some individuals may prefer one way of dealing with a situation to another. Each individual may well have a constituency and it may be necessary to bargain and compromise in order to reach mutually acceptable decisions. Each individual coming to the decision-making process is representative, to a greater or lesser degree, of a number of environmental elements. Social interaction among individuals both within and outside the work situation is also an influence. Other internal factors include the economic and technological environments within which one works.

Many libraries today exist on the edge of penury. Others have suffered and continue to suffer from budget cutbacks. Money is rarely available in sufficient quantity and a condition of genteel poverty and make-do may result. This attitude will influence decision-making. If the library is in a situation that permits economic growth and development, that too will influence attitudes and decisions.

The success and speed with which technology has been incorporated into library operations will affect reactions toward additional proposals for upgrade of systems, increased networking, enhanced access to information systems, etc. If technological changes have been carefully considered and planning has been conducted with the participants, both staff and clientele, in mind, there will be a greater willingness to continue to move at a steady pace toward the kind of library we need to construct for the next decades.

Each participant in the process has a different value system—in fact two value systems: a personal value system and an organizational value system, and there will be interaction between the two. Each individual has a different amount of power and a different commitment to past directions. These all constitute irrational decision-making inputs and it is often on the basis of such factors rather than techniques such as operations research and systems analysis that decisions are made.[2]

Any decision-making situation is subject to conflicting expectations among those involved in the process. Increasing the library's support for outreach programs may be in conflict with the objectives of those who wish to enhance CD ROM networks in support of the reference service capacity of the library. When funds are limited and priorities must be set, conflicts between groups with specific interests arise; there may also be conflict between individuals. Problems do not exist in a vacuum; they are linked to other situations. It may be necessary to choose between two courses of action or to deal with one problem before dealing with the other.

STRUCTURE FOR BUDGET-MAKING

The actual budgeting process is under the overall direction of the library director, who may supervise activities or may delegate that responsibility to an assistant who in turn may delegate further to an assistant who in turn may control or delegate. What is essential is that there be a carefully determined plan for allocating responsibility, gathering data, and making decisions, all within reasonable time constraints.

For a number of years there has been discussion of the extent to which those who are responsible for performance under the budget should be involved in the budget decision-making process. The advantages of broader participation are that there will be a greater understanding of both possibilities and constraints, and that a stronger link will be forged between the operator and institutional goals. The extent to which various individuals are included in the process will depend upon a number of factors, including their knowledge of operations and services, their experience, and their interests. The more participation there is, the longer it will take to arrive at decisions. This disadvantage must be balanced against the value of group consensus. The less sophisticated in management in general and information management in particular that the participants are, the more initial educational time must be spent. Here again one must balance long-term benefit against short-term inconvenience.

The process, first and foremost, is based on sharing information in an environment of cooperation. Leadership must be provided by the library director, budget officer or committee charged with the task, and that leadership should be constructive rather than restrictive. The process follows the budget cycle and is the means by which that cycle is implemented. It begins with the establishment of long-range goals or a review of existing goals. From these, annual goals are developed and refined, and on the basis of these goals both the long-range and the annual financial plan are constructed. Part of the planning process is an exploration of alternatives, alternatives in setting priorities among objectives and alternatives in levels of their funding. Each of these requires broad discussion, with staff sharing fully in the process of determining which goals are most important and which should receive priority attention.

Everyone involved in the process must be aware of and understand the assumptions used in planning for and projecting revenue and expenditure so that the reasons for cutting back on spending or for an unexpected extra bit of income are clearly understood. Financial management is often viewed as inexplicable and secret, and reductions in funds as the result of poor management. This may be true in some cases, but more often it is the result of changes in anticipated revenue, something over which the library manager has little or no control. Keeping staff members informed of the true status of revenues gives them a better understanding of resources available and goes a long way toward insuring their support in times of crisis.

In addition to participative decision-making and open communication, the process must be supported by a strong financial accounting and budgeting system. The system within the library must be in accord with that of the larger organization of which the library is a part. In many academic institutions, associations, and business enterprises a strong overall budgeting and accounting system exists. In most local governments, too, sound budgeting and accounting systems exist, but there are local government systems which are in need of review and revision. Because of the political factors that arise in reorganizing local government accounting systems, change tends to be slow. In such an environment it may be necessary for the library to devise its own internal system in order to monitor its activities. In this instance, this internal system operates in addition to the system mandated by local government. As local government systems become more professional and more highly automated, the need for backup systems will disappear.

The budget and accounting system should be constructed in such a way that the information necessary to evaluate the library's financial condition is available in usable form on a regular basis. This information should be available not only to the budget officer but also to the individuals carrying out the programs that are being monitored, so that they can contribute to and interpret the evaluative data.

PROMOTING CHANGE IN AN ORGANIZATION

There are no measurable factors that specifically quantify readiness for change. There are, however, indications of readiness for change as well as rules for organizing the change process. Basic to the process is an understanding of the organization as it is, its systems and processes, and the attitudes of individuals. One also needs to understand the strategies that can be used to implement and carry out change, such as the role of leadership and the politics of interaction within the organization. Although much research has been conducted in an attempt to identify change agents and processes, there are no firm rules as to how to implement change. The change process is the most nebulous of managerial activities.

Change can be achieved through the adoption of new ideas, methods, or technology. The redesign of reference service to take into consideration the availability of information on the Internet or the purchase of access to electronic journals are examples of specific change decisions. Although the fact of change is tied to a specific event, the decisions leading up to the change may have been initiated at a number of levels in addition to that of the manager. The speed with which new or additional ways of doing things are adopted is dependent in large part on the environment. Individuals who have a stake in their jobs and feel responsible for improving their work, those who see technological and organizational change as beneficial and the administration as welcoming new ideas, are more geared to change.

In the area of financial planning, change is usually motivated by the lack of adequate resources to achieve objectives that have been accomplished in the past. The need to choose among objectives or to do things in most cost-effective ways requires a rethinking of current activities. For some, this situation results in a strategic planning process in which the entire organization is analyzed in relation to its mission, and from this analysis goals and objectives are set and prioritized. For others, the decision may be to reduce some activities, eliminate some, and perhaps enhance others. For those institutions which experience repeated cuts in their resources, the gradual reduction and reprioritization of services becomes more and more difficult to do. Eventually, they will undertake a strategic planning process which may well result in a restructure or a refocused organization. The change process should be studied carefully in light of the existing situation in the organization. The library that maintains appropriate evaluative measures describing its services, their cost and the trend of each, is in a better position to identify activities that should be reviewed. There is no single solution to any problem area. The library director or staff member may see one set of variables and identify a certain course of action. A consultant may use the same data and suggest a different course of action. It is the analysis of various options that will usually result in the most appropriate course of action. An obvious problem may be only an indication that there is a larger problem. The library that is running out of shelf space has an immediate storage problem but the underlying problem may be lack of financial support from the parent institution that has slowed efforts toward the building of a much-needed new library. This in turn may be a symptom of the economic status of the parent institution and the state of the economy. A lack of shelf space may also be due to a reluctance on the part of some to rethink the ways in which information is acquired and used, with the result that the balance between information available from books and that available through electronic access is too heavily slanted in the direction of books. This may signal the need to provide collection development and reference personnel with additional opportunities to become comfortable with electronic formats.

Whatever changes are recommended, they must be relevant to the history and purpose of the organization. An academic library whose major purpose is support of the curriculum cannot suddenly open its doors and become a community agency with the functions of a public library. The collections are different, as are the types of services provided. Major changes in orientation can and do occur but they must develop deliberately and with understanding. Change must take into account the larger environment in which the organization exists.

Planned change includes the appropriate crafting, to the extent possible, of the environment so that change will be welcome. This may include staff discussion of the need to revise procedures to adopt a new program or to cut back on the budget. It may even mean a more radical shift such as combining two types of information organizations. If this occurs there are major ramifications. If, for example, an academic library plans to open its doors to the community at large, what effect will this have on the other information sources available to the community—the public library, specialized information services, the school media center? What is the attitude of staff toward the new clientele? What legislation exists that may affect the proposed change? Serious change affects both organizational structure and individual attitudes. Being aware of both the positive and negative implications of change permits those who are making decisions and supervising activities to develop means of easing the stress that tends to accompany the introduction of new ways of doing things.

In any situation some things are more easily changed than others. When planning the budget, salary items are often set by law or by the larger organization of which the library is a part. Staff members may have tenure and must be retained. There is little the director can do to reduce or hold the line on salary items other than letting people go or not filling positions. If the budget requires a cut in program, factors that can be changed must be identified. A frequent result is that materials are reduced and supplies cut because these are factors under the control of the local unit. Because non-staff items are the easiest to change, non-innovative planners may hack away at the materials budget as the simplest way to reduce costs. In the long run this may be more costly than reallocation of personnel or changes in organizational structure. Although it is relatively easy to identify factors one can label as manipulable, this is not a sufficient or satisfactory method of identifying change procedures or areas. Change must be effective in actually solving problems. If a new approach does not deal with the situation under consideration in a positive fashion, why make the change?

COMMUNICATION IN BUDGET MAKING

Managed change is the product of planning. Neither change nor planning, however, can be implemented without clear communication within the organization and open channels with external agencies. Whether the communication network transmits budget or other types of information, it is a critical element in any organization.

> Communication of budgeted goals downward in an organiza-
> tion informs members of lower management what upper
> management expects of them; conversely, upper management
> learns about the accomplishments and problems of lower
> management through upward flowing reports comparing
> budgeted goals with actual performance.[3]

The vehicle for communication may be planning, budgeting, evaluation, or some other activity requiring cooperation at various levels. In fact, any single vehicle carries with it elements of other activities. The budgeting process depends in large measure upon the goals and objectives of an organization as determined through planning sessions. It depends as well upon the evaluative measures developed to determine the progress toward objectives, and accountability measures developed to determine how well funds were spent. There is an added element, personnel concerns: the extent to which the organization considers the individual and the factors that motivate the individual to perform at an optimum level.

The extent to which the budgeting process is an effective conduit for communication is determined in large part by the attitudes of those traditionally responsible for budgeting activities. The library director, the department heads or other members of the administrative group may find it difficult to share the budget-making process with members of their staff. This may be due to an unwillingness to share authority, a comfort with old authoritarian structures which are no longer generally acceptable, a reluctance to complicate a process already in place, or insecurity about dealing with the real possibility that associates will question decisions. Within even the most participatory situation those who have traditionally been charged with planning can so structure the activity that there is little real opportunity for contributions from staff members. The extent and form of participation can be controlled by the amount of feedback provided, and by its timing.

Kenis conducted a study of the relationship of budgetary planning to managerial attitudes. His review of the literature identified current thinking on budgetary participation: that individuals involved in goal setting are more willing to work toward those goals than those who have had goals thrust upon them. They feel better about their jobs and about the organization in which they work. They may not work harder but their attitudes are more positive. Individuals who understand the organizational goals clearly are more able to work toward meeting them. Feedback, particularly in budgetary terms, is most important because it not only provides an indication of current fiscal status but evaluative data on the relationship between the amount of money spent and the progress toward goals. There appears to be a tendency in many organizations for one or two individuals in managerial positions to be highly secretive about current financial status. The reason may be lack of understanding of the importance of keeping staff apprised of the way in which funds are spent, or an authoritarian attitude on the part of a manager who sees control of the purse strings as a means of maintaining control over staff. Communication within the library is an "ongoing process of generating, transmitting and receiving information related to the organization's purposes. The process is influenced by the availability and use of formal established channels, general library climate, individual communication skills, and the quality and nature of inter-personal relationships."[4]

Although internal budget planning and decision-making are concerned with priority setting within an organization and the allocation of resources within the priority scheme, they are at all times linked to such external factors as the economy, political necessity, the current state of information technology, and the needs of information users. Knowing how to plan, how to plan for change and how to communicate, both within the organization and outside it, are critical to the development of a useful and usable budget.

NOTES

1. Izzettin Kenis, "Effects of Budgetary Goal Characteristics on Managerial Attitudes and Performance." *The Accounting Review* 54:4, October, 1979, p.707.
2. K. J. Radford, *Complex Decision Problems; An Integrated Strategy for Resolution.* Reston, Va.: Reston Publishing Co., 1977.
3. Kenis, p. 707.
4. Association of Research Libraries, "Internal Communication: Policies and Procedures." *Systems Procedures Exchange Center Kit #54.* Washington, D.C.: The Association, May 1979, p.1

IV.

DATA GATHERING METHODOLOGIES

Data gathering is not decision-making but is a necessary prior step. Before making budget decisions, many questions need to be answered. How much does a service cost? How many people use the service? What is the average cost of a book, a journal, a videotape? What is the impact of legislation or administrative decisions on salary levels or expectations of services? Cost of maintenance, of utilities and of communications must also be determined. Many of these and related data are available from sources within the library or information center.

Although library personnel are information specialists, they tend to short-change their own information gathering needs. They often do not place the organization and management of information needed to operate their service at a particularly high priority level. Either they work with relatively little management data, or large amounts of information are collected, the purpose of which may be vague. It is often the case that the means of data collection and representation are not uniform. The purpose of the data may be to improve internal management or to satisfy external data collection needs, such as the requirements of a municipal administration or university budget office. If it is the latter, data collection is often designed with that single purpose in mind and with relatively little thought given to multiple purposes the information could serve.

Not-for-profit organizations, unlike their for-profit colleagues, have a shorter history of analyzing the data they collect, due in part to limited expertise in data analysis. Until recently, too few library managers and planners were comfortable with basic statistical techniques or understood the value of such analysis to the improvement of their operations. Because of the amount of data libraries collect but often do not analyze for use, they are among those organizations called "data rich but information poor."[1]

59

SOURCES OF PLANNING DATA

Planning documents and minutes of board and committee meetings serve as the basis for planning the budget, as they indicate the direction the institution is to take, set priorities for action, and indicate the relative balance of these priorities. Documents from outside the library are also to be consulted in order to determine the context within which the library's plan for the next year(s) is placed. The accounts and records of the library or information service provide essential background material for developing the budget, if records are in order and past budgets and studies are available. In some libraries, the level and quality of record-keeping has not been adequate. Where the institutional budgeting history is unavailable or incomplete, the development of the budget is more difficult.

The financial planning process has several cycles, one of them being the planning, budgeting, spending, reporting cycle in which the information used to conduct the budgeting activity for one year is used to plan for the ensuing year or years. In this model, reporting systems should be devised in such a fashion that they provide efficient planning data organized to assist the individual planning unit and are at the same time compatible with all other units in the library and in the larger organization of which the library is a part. A major reason for the review of reporting procedures by external experts is to ascertain that the library's record-keeping is in accord with that of the larger institution and with the standards of the accounting profession.

To obtain those kinds of information not easily accessible from library records or from directives, memos and other communication, a number of data gathering methodologies are available. Methodologies such as unit costing, benchmarking, cost analyses and cost benefit analyses are regularly used by management to collect and analyze data for decision-making. In themselves they do not provide answers to questions but they do provide input for identifying alternatives.

UNIT COSTS

Cost is defined as a monetary measure of the amount of resources used for a particular purpose. Unit cost is the amount of resources used to produce one unit for a particular purpose. For example, how much does it cost to process one book, to circulate one book, to answer a reference question from print sources, from on-line sources? These are production cost measures and relate cost to the production of a good or a service.

To determine a unit cost, the procedure is to divide the total cost of producing a specified number of units by the number of units produced. The result is a figure that represents the average cost of production per unit. The formula for this is:

$$\text{Unit Cost} = \frac{\text{Cost of Producing N Units}}{\text{N}}$$

The unit cost serves as a means of comparing the cost of producing a unit, for example the cost of processing a book, from year to year in the same library or among libraries. One can determine whether such an activity is increasing in cost or whether one library is able to fulfill the task more economically than another. It is also possible to determine whether one way of carrying out the activity is less costly than another. Benchmarking "an ongoing, systematic process for measuring and comparing the work processes of one organization to those of another by bringing an external focus to the internal activities, functions or operations"[2] provides an external standard for evaluating one's own processes and identifies those organizations and processes one wishes to emulate. Using unit costing to determine one's own costs and relating them to the benchmarked information from institutions conducting like processes allows the library manager to plan activities on the basis of data showing how different procedures affect cost. Unit cost development serves as the basis for cost analysis.

Personnel—Information services are highly labor-intensive and personnel costs constitute the largest single component of a unit cost. The cost that is factored in includes both salary and benefits. Of the approximately forty hours per week for which an employee is paid, a percentage includes time used for vacation, for sick leave, and for times during the work day when the employee is at lunch or otherwise occupied in non-job related activities. Unit cost therefore is calculated based on actual number of hours worked, plus benefits. The resulting productive hourly cost may be as much as one-third higher than the hourly wage before time not spent in actual work is factored out. If the hourly wage of a cataloger on an annual basis (before benefits are added) is twenty dollars, when time not actually working is factored out, the resulting salary may be closer to twenty-eight dollars per hour. The cost of supervision and training and other interpersonal activities necessary to a job—such as staff meetings, meeting with vendors, and similar activities—are also added to the labor cost.

Because of the need for cooperation in the costing effort and the implied threat that one is "being checked up on," cost studies are most successfully conducted in an atmosphere of mutual understanding and trust. The authoritarian manager who announces that cost studies will be conducted and that each staff member will, for a stated period of time, record all use of time, will be met with resentment and less than full cooperation. The manager who has a good working relation with staff and who involves them in the planning process will be more successful in developing and implementing time studies. In either case, a measure of education is necessary so that staff members will understand the need to determine as closely as possible the cost of an activity and the relationship between this and overall planning, priority setting, and budgeting. Although an element of employee evaluation may be implicit in the process, this should be downplayed in the time-study process because here the emphasis is upon how long it actually takes to complete a task and the average time needed for completion.

Other information useful to the manager is bound to emerge from such time studies. For example, it may be determined that the reference specialist is answering too many directional questions that could better be answered by a support person receiving a lower salary, or that a department head is preparing routine reports that could be done more economically by a clerical staff person. It is often during a time study that a chronically overworked staff member discovers the reason for his or her job burden; it may be poor organization of tasks, the assumption of unnecessary tasks, or too comprehensive a job description. It is often for such related kinds of information that a time study, whose primary purpose is to determine costs, can be promoted.

Depreciation—In addition to labor costs, the cost of depreciation of equipment must be included in the unit cost. All equipment, from typewriters to work stations to calculators to desks, chairs, and filing cabinets, has an average usable lifespan, usually between five and ten years. For accounting purposes, a percentage of the replacement cost of each item should be a part of the cost of performing tasks. For example, if one expects to get five years of service from a work station, twenty per cent of its replacement cost should be considered as an annual cost. This can cause difficulties in the not-for-profit agency, where putting funds aside to replace the equipment is not possible in a budget that must be spent annually with no carry-over. For the purpose of ascertaining actual unit costs, however, depreciation has to be figured in.

A number of depreciation models exist by which it is possible to determine what the appropriate rate of depreciation is for particular kinds of equipment. The two most common models are straight line depreciation and declining balance depreciation. The simplest model, straight line, is calculated in the following manner:

$$\text{Annual amount} = \frac{\text{purchase price} - \text{salvage value of item when replaced}}{\text{number of years between the time the item was purchased and was replaced}}$$

For example, a new IBM work station costs \$2500 and will be replaced in five years. Annual depreciation is \$400.

$$\frac{2500 - 500 \text{ (salvage value)}}{5} = \frac{2000}{5} \text{ or \$400 per year}$$

The straight line depreciation method assumes that the work station will decline in value by an equal amount each year. In fact, the equipment will decline in value more during the early years and less thereafter. Automobiles are valued by the declining balance method, where depreciation is high in the first year or two, declines slowly thereafter and levels off when the car is toward the end of its useful life. Different items depreciate at different rates and a number of schedules need to be set up to take these differences into account.

What is not factored into either of these methods is the actual replacement cost as affected by inflation. The cost of replacing the work station when it has reached the end of its useful life will most likely be higher than the original purchase price. In the case of computing equipment, the decreasing cost of components may offset inflation to a degree. Other items, such as furniture and equipment other than computing equipment, will not be affected by these potential decreasing costs and the full impact of inflation must be factored in.

Work stations, furniture and other similar equipment depreciate because they wear out or become unusable. Setting a replacement schedule for such items is relatively easy. Books and other informational materials depreciate as well, but in different ways. Some reference materials are annuals and must be replaced each year. Other materials provide retrospective information or are primarily literary and their contents do not become outdated. A large percentage of the collection may become outdated as new information becomes available through scientific discoveries, political changes, or other influences. Information requires constant updating. In addition, bindings become worn, paper deteriorates, and standard editions of heavily used materials wear out because of heavy use.

This issue received considerable discussion as a result of Ruling 93 by the Financial Accounting Standards Board, which requires that not-for-profit organizations recognize depreciation. This 1987 ruling covers collections such as those owned by libraries, galleries, museums and botanical gardens.[3] A study done under a Cooperative Research Grant from the Council on Library Resources concluded that ". . . the best approach [to factoring depreciation] is to determine the useful life of the . . . library materials, on a class by class basis and then apply a practical means of recognizing depreciation that is fairly representative of actual use patterns."[4]

Continuing with unit cost calculation, maintenance of leased equipment, including subscriptions to CD-ROM and similar on-line reference services, must be included as a cost in all programs in which they are used. If work stations are leased, those costs are part of the cost of providing the service. If automobiles or service vans are leased, these too are included in the costing of services for which they are used. Costs of supplies such as paper, pens, discs, etc. are relatively easy to identify and to assign. The cost of storing supplies and housing any finished products such as bibliographies, reports or newsletter publications is a final item to be calculated in determining unit costs.

Physical Plant—The library building, or a percentage of a larger building in which the library is housed, is also figured into unit costs. The cost per square foot of replacing the building, figured on the basis of a twenty-year life, plus the cost per square foot of insurance, cleaning and other maintenance, heating, security and other costs of keeping the building in shape are all part of the unit costs. On an annual basis, it is desirable to figure the overall cost of maintaining the building and from this to calculate a per square foot cost. When looking at a particular activity to determine its unit cost, the number of square feet taken up by the activity is multiplied by the maintenance cost per square foot. In the case of such activities as the maintenance of stacks and cost for storage per volume, this represents a major portion of the cost; for labor-intensive activities such as verification of citations, space costs are a minor element in the overall cost. If a building is rented or leased, the per square foot costs are based on annual rental and any maintenance costs not included in that rental.

Fixed and Variable Costs—Two additional sets of costs need to be identified in the planning/budgeting process: fixed costs and variable costs. A fixed cost is one which does not vary with varying amounts of service. Fixed costs include the cost of keeping a library open regardless of the volume of business, or of providing a program regardless of the number of people who take advantage of it. Variable costs are those that change depending upon the number of activities involved or the number of people taking advantage of the service. A simplistic example would be a pre-school story hour. Fixed costs would be the cost of the location of the story telling, the salary of the story teller, and the cost of the book and other story-telling aids. For an audience of one child or a hundred children, these costs would be the same. If apples were to be given out after the story was told and if they were worth ten cents apiece, the cost for an audience of one child would be a dime, but if a hundred showed up the cost would be ten dollars. The total apple cost varies with the number of users.

Building Block Costing—One method of developing cost data for information activities, building block costing, relies on the development of units of measure for each activity. The information activity is divided and subdivided into subsystems, each of which can be measured as a single unit. Each unit must be countable and the count verifiable. For example, each task in an indexing activity is identified and a means of counting the times a task is performed is established.[5] Another understanding in building block costing is that unit costs are useful only within the context of all system costs. As an information service is analyzed, certain aspects and activities will defy assignment for cost purposes. To obtain accurate cost figures, however, they must be included in total costs. One means of doing this is to lump them in one group and provide a gross unit cost for these items alone, adding that gross unit cost to each of the more carefully derived unit cost figures.

A final premise of building block costing, Price stresses, is that valid unit costs must be derived from sufficient information to permit statistical analysis, and that the data must have been collected within a normal operating environment rather than in a specifically developed test situation. The cost of the activity must be related to the actual production resulting from expenditure. This can be realized only when actual work situations are studied.

Benefits of Developing Unit Cost Data—Calculating unit costs serves a number of purposes. The most evident is that the actual cost of performing a service or completing a task can be determined. A further benefit is that in the process of identifying unit costs, the manager/planner looks very carefully at each element of cost and may find that the cost of materials or of staff time in performing the task is out of line. Adjustments can then be made so that the task can be accomplished in a more economical fashion.

As mentioned earlier, the unit cost is the basic element of cost accounting. It provides a measure against which comparisons can be made of the cost of alternative ways of completing tasks and with the cost of completing like tasks in other institutions. Maintaining and updating unit costs over a period provides information on how the cost of completing a task has increased in response to inflation or has decreased as a result of technological innovation or task redesign. It serves as a building block for planning and the development of detailed budgets.

Limitations of Developing Unit Cost Data—The concept of unit costs is based on the premise that it is possible to identify and describe discrete units of library and information service in the same manner as it is possible to determine the exact cost to a bakery of producing a loaf of bread of a certain size and shape and wrapped for sale. In a service industry, and information service falls in this area, such is not the case because services provided are more sensitive than products are to the demands and needs of the clientele. An on-line searching service may have been studied carefully to determine costs, average work load, and anticipated development. A sudden surge of activity, a change in software, a change in content of the data base or an evaluation study such as the cost study itself may temporarily skew the cost figures that have been developed. In nearly all cases of unit costing of information services, one should view the resulting figures as a good general approximation rather than as exact. They are sufficiently valid to provide general answers to such managerial questions as the percentage of cost represented by labor, whether the nature of the job permits a lower salaried staff member to perform parts of it, or what effect increased or reduced units of work would have on cost.

An unsatisfactory means of allocating cost is to take the total expenditure of a department or unit for a year and divide it by a unit of activity. For example, the cost of running a circulation service is divided by the number of books and other materials circulated, or the cost of a children's program by the number of children served. The results of such a method are unusable; there is no identification of variables, only a gross lumping together of all costs divided by an available user figure. Those who use this method often go a step further and use it as a measure of productivity for an entire department. This is particularly suspect; it is just not possible to measure total productivity from such poorly defined figures. Those who are inexperienced in planning or in politics may assume that such figures have merit. If they use them, they do so at their peril.

COST ACCOUNTING

Cost accounting, the identification of the cost of providing specific services, is a management tool involving the entire organization. Although its major focus is financial, its implications are broader. Its purpose is to tie effectiveness to cost so that the resulting information can be used for comparisons of the cost of similar activities within the organization and among similar organizations.

Cost studies for library and information services begin with the assumption that they are useful and indeed serve a purpose. Most libraries and information services perform the same general functions and can be compared on this basis. It is in the identification of specific tasks that variations occur, although a number of tasks may be performed in similar ways. Tasks within a library or information center need to be analyzed to determine the interrelationships that exist among them. The purpose of such studies is not to establish standards or norms but simply to identify costs within an organization at a particular time.

Studies to determine the actual cost of a program or activity have long been used as a tool in the for-profit sector and have long been resisted by those who provide services rather than goods, particularly those who are funded through taxes, donations or other sources not directly related to the cost of the product or service itself. It has often been said that one cannot put a price on the cost of providing information to a client or the cost of providing a story hour or reader's advisory service. In the sense that the value of the interpersonal interchange cannot be priced this is true, but it is not true that one cannot determine the cost in staff time and resources used.

The development of a cost analysis program for a library or other information center follows generally accepted guidelines but requires some tailoring to the specific situation. Because of the need to develop the program on site, it may well be best developed by an internal staff member or someone who knows the organization well, assisted by an external consultant, rather than by an external consultant alone. It is also important to have one individual responsible for cost analysis study within the organization.

The methodology for conducting the cost analysis begins with an identification of all library activities currently being performed. They are then grouped by major task category and broad functions are identified. Tasks are then assigned to appropriate functions. Organizational units for which costs are to be determined are established. Production units produced by the library are defined and equated to standard units. A system of computer programs is then developed to provide regular reports of cost.

As an example, Mitchell et al.[6] identified five units within the academic library. The *processing production unit* has volumes added as the basic unit. Processing time figures are converted to volumes-added figures for other items. It is possible to determine the tasks and the time required to add one volume. Other items processed receive similar attention and are then converted to volumes-added equivalents. The *reference service production unit* is based on the average time for each traditional question category: directional, consultation, equipment. Additional production units include *interlibrary loan, circulation production units,* based on one item circulated as the base unit; and the *library instruction production unit,* with the number of patrons instructed as the base unit, or the number of bibliographies developed amortized over the number of years they are used. Although this work was done some time ago, the basic units continue to work well. Within the units, tasks will have changed because of changes in technology, management and approaches to the activity.

When one attempts to group activities under tasks, variances between tasks as described and actual performance of them become apparent. Tasks as written down represent a static situation; the actual performance may have changed over time in response to changed need. The task as written may be too theoretical to translate into actual performance. Often, a great deal of adaptation is necessary to merge activities and tasks. As noted earlier, the cost activity has major implications in other areas such as work-flow patterns and job descriptions.

Conducting cost studies has been seen by more and more libraries as a useful management tool. A number of cost studies have been conducted in major academic libraries, either to identify costs to be allocated to research or to develop cost-flow studies in order to justify budget increases to university administrators. As budgets become constricted, the cost study provides a means of more precisely identifying the effects of inadequate funding.

The library is a cost center within the larger organization and is subject to the levels of accountability applied to all other cost centers. Because two-thirds or more of a library budget typically consists of personnel cost, the majority of the data needed to justify cost must be in support of the need for staff. Cost studies may reveal certain activities which have unusually high costs and may lead to adjustments in the way those tasks are performed. If tasks are redesigned to reduce costs, workloads may change in the process, or the organization of a department may be modified and other personnel-related decisions made. Information derived from cost studies is useful in forecasting and this, related to an analysis of the current economic situation and probable trends, provides as useful a combination of financial planning data as it is possible to obtain. This is likely to be a more accurate means of projecting increases than is the addition of a standard inflation figure to each item or program.

As more and more libraries adopt program budgeting and therefore need to know what the costs of their services are, careful review of activities becomes essential. The availability of management information system software allows us to receive, on a regular basis, output data on units of work produced. Care must be taken to insure that the data generated are the data needed for the process. Too often, such software is installed without careful attention having been paid to the relationship between what it can produce and what is needed for planning. Generating data in this manner is a useful and cost efficient means of monitoring activity.

COST BENEFIT ANALYSIS

In any decision-making process, there are certain common elements, beginning with the definition of the problem and the determination of the desired objective. Controlling variables are identified and the best alternative is selected as the means of working through the decision process. A clear identification of the goals and objectives of the unit and the resources available for implementation is required. Cost-benefit analysis is a method of identifying not only the costs of a program or activity but also the benefits of each alternative. Deciding "is the product worth the price?" is both objective in terms of dollar figures and subjective because of the determination of value. It is necessary to ask which activity or direction is best both in terms of cost input and benefit output. Behind each decision is the assumption of net gain, though each is part of a continuum of collective decisions which should be consistent with the objectives of the library. A number of intangibles are present in the cost-benefit process and even through they cannot be assigned a direct dollar value, they represent aspects of the financial health of the organization.

The decisions made in regard to the expenditure of money can have an impact on the image projected by the library. Does the library make decisions that seem to serve one clientele in preference to others? Does there seem to be a reluctance to move aggressively into electronic access? Is the building dull, dingy and uninviting because of poor maintenance? There may be valid reasons for making specific decisions, but the decisions themselves and their collective impact will to a large extent label the library and its services as either innovative and forward-thinking or traditional—or perhaps somewhere in between.

Financial decisions can also affect staff morale. The staff member who has worked to design a new expert system to assist students in finding their way around a complex library will respond positively if that activity is funded and will doubtless work hard to make it a success. This attitude is likely to spill over into other activities and the staff member will work at a high level of performance. Conversely, the staff member whose plans and programs are consistently under-funded or not funded at all may not put as much effort into working and may well become discouraged. The impact of such levels of satisfaction and dissatisfaction will produce a general staff attitude. When decisions are made that seem to the staff to represent the best allocation of funds, staff will support them even when overall funding is low. If there appears to be favoritism in allocating funds, with specific programs or individuals receiving or appearing to receive an undue share of resources, staff will object. The manager needs to be prepared to show cost figures to support decisions or to conduct cost studies promptly. The extent to which the library manager allocates funds in support of the library's program in a fair and businesslike manner will determine to a large degree the attitude of staff toward the quality of management. One of the ways a library's priority in the larger organization can be determined is the level of support it receives. Similarly, within an organization, staff will assess their own priority roles in terms of the funds they receive.

The results of information service, because it deals to a large extent in intangibles (the quality of information, the intellectual effort required, use of the information gained, and satisfaction of the client), are to a large degree not measurable in dollars. Nevertheless it is both possible and necessary to use dollar figures as one way of measuring library service and of setting priorities. It is by the use of such measures that some cherished things done in libraries may be found to cost too much or to be too little used.

Another purpose of cost-benefit studies is to identify levels of service. How much information does a client need? Is there such a thing as too much information? What is the break point between enough and too much service? As our clientele becomes increasingly diverse, costs of service tend to increase. It may be more costly to provide service to a physically disabled individual who may need additional support in order to obtain information in a format which is useful for her or his needs. It may also be more costly to provide materials in more than one language or at different levels of difficulty. It is important to identify the costs of the range of services available to meet diverse needs. It is also necessary to keep uppermost in one's mind that quality service to all who have the right to use a library is fundamental to the mission of the library and the information professions, even though the cost of serving diverse needs will be higher than if only a single basic level of service were available.

Cost-benefit has been defined as the "ratio of the amount of money collected from customers to the total funding for the information service."[7] This assumes that a charge of some sort accompanies each service and, if the system is to be self-supporting, the income must equal cost. In the not-for-profit sector, cost-benefit is calculated differently: the costs of an activity are identified, often unit cost is determined, and a decision is then made as to whether the cost to the taxpayer is unduly high. If it is, some reductions in cost input must be considered, or programs may be eliminated, or, because of overriding social or educational benefit, certain programs may be funded despite the cost.

There is a basic assumption in some circles that the library, by definition, is a good thing and that its benefits are not to be questioned. Although this is a comfortable assumption, it is unwise for library personnel to allow it to go unchallenged, particularly in the face of scarce resources. Because an institution is respected and its services considered essential to the community it serves, there is no assurance that it will be funded at a reasonable level. The information community should do its own studies and make its own decisions prior to external challenges by those who control funding. Although the public or academic library is unlikely to be shut down entirely because of failure to justify its services, this can and does happen elsewhere. As funding for schools is reduced, many school libraries have had their services reduced or eliminated. Given the availability of information at the work station, many for-profit agencies have assumed that they no longer need an information professional or a library and have closed the company library. As resources decline, one needs to have hard data to support the value of the library or information center to the child's education or to the success of a business enterprise.

The for-profit organization is more likely to be managed by professional managers than is the non-profit environment and these individuals may not be swayed by arguments justifying library service on the grounds that it is educationally, socially, or intellectually useful. They are concerned with its relationship to company profits. In the for-profit environment, information service is typically classified as overhead, its services being generally available rather than tied to a particular project. There is some question as to whether it is possible to assign viable cost figures to library service in such a setting.

Those who have done studies of the projected cost of information required to conduct a research project have indicated generally what those costs would be. The assumption is that a specific level of service or amount of data is provided and that either can be costed out. From the vantage point of individual activity, it may be possible to cost out information for a project. Combining the costs of individual projects does not necessarily provide a complete picture of the library when it is placed in the category of general overhead. Some educated guesses may be made but hard data is difficult to develop.

The Cost-Benefit Study: "The major objective of a cost benefit analysis is to determine the economic feasibility of developing alternatives to the current system. It insures that the user receives the best possible return for the investment."[8]

Several years ago the Virginia Beach, Virginia Public Library conducted a study to determine the economic feasibility of automating catalog production and maintenance. The goals identified for the automation project were: the conversion of the public catalog from printed card form to a magnetic tape/disc, a storage/retrieval system with COM (Computer Output Microform) access, and automation of library circulation and control routines and procedures. These products would be used for development of a regional library information network. The data processing department devised a methodology to provide needed information, beginning with a study of library manual routines, specifically card production and maintenance. They then assisted in the establishment of a phased approach to conversion to assure compatibility among phases as the work progressed. At this point, most of the activity centered around the need to identify the procedures involved in catalog production and maintenance: who was involved, what the interrelationships of these activities were within the library, and what impact changes would have on city-wide data processing resources to which library data processing was tied. Identification of all aspects of the new process was followed by assignment of appropriate costs.

The cost of the present card production and maintenance system and of two alternatives were determined. A turnkey system was the least costly alternative. An in-house system plus a COM catalog from an outside source had a costly start-up figure but costs after the first year were lower. The existing system was found to be the most costly. In addition to cost figures, the benefits of an automated system in terms of access sites and the elimination of the cost of maintaining the card catalog were considered. From among the three options, it was then possible to select one on the basis of identified objectives, cost calculations, and anticipated benefits. A decision to eliminate the least costly option, were it to lack many of the benefits of a more expensive option, could be justified. Benefits to the library in terms of better record keeping or more efficient maintenance, or such benefits to patrons as greater access, could be stressed, depending upon the audience being informed of the proposed decision.

Cost analysis and its accompanying cost-benefit factor have value beyond the identification of costs. The process requires that library staff examine closely how they perform a task and what factors are involved. It is often this review and analysis that is the most important aspect of the costing process.

Cost-Benefit Analyses of the Library within Its Community: As current cost decisions have to be effected in future environments, projections must attempt to take into account external environmental factors over which the library manager has little or no control, such as a decline in statewide revenue which might require reductions in a budget already approved, or a larger than anticipated inflationary increase in materials costs. A decline in enrollment at a college or university or a movement to the suburbs of members of the public library's clientele will change the library's support base as well as its user group and workload.

Mason,[9] in discussing a cost-benefit model for information services, has differentiated between the private and social costs of an activity. A private cost is what a person or an organization gives in order to receive a good or a service; a social cost is what society must give up in order to permit the individual to receive the good or the service. In many cases the private and social costs are similar. For example, the cost of a book to a buyer may be equivalent to the cost of producing the book—the consumer has paid the full price for the item. In other cases, such as the provision of public housing, society subsidizes the service and the consumer pays directly for only a part of that service. Information services fall into the latter category. In most cases they are subsidized through taxes and any direct cost to the user is a minor part of the actual cost. This is a reflection of the concept of the library as a public good. It represents something society is willing to pay for in order to make the social environment more satisfying. The costs associated with providing information services are the resources given up by society in order for the service to be offered. These include staff costs, utilities, supplies, and the cost of the informational materials.

Benefits are measured by willingness to pay, but there are few available data on what society or the individual is willing to give up in order to have information service. The ability to pay and, to an extent, the willingness to pay can be determined partially by the priority level that library service receives when budgets of the community, the college or university, or other agency are determined. A high value is often set on the need for information, but there may nevertheless be an unwillingness to pay for the service. When fees are charged to cover part of the cost of making information available, there is typically a sharp drop in use. Mason, in developing his cost-benefit model for information services, indicated that it is difficult to collect useful data on benefits because of the difficulty of separating the value of the service that provides information from the value of the information itself. He concluded that there is no way to measure the actual social benefits of information or information service, although it is generally accepted that those benefits exist.

In addition to the allocation of resources, who benefits from library and information services? Does one group benefit to a greater degree than others? Is the group that benefits the group that pays? In the case of public library services, the typical user has been described as middle class and middle income. Since the bulk of the support of the public library comes from local taxes, is the middle-income family paying its share for library support? What about the residents who are taxed for use but do not use the service? This is a frequently voiced argument and the usual response is that the taxpayer derives general benefits from taxes but does not benefit in equal measure from all tax-supported services. However, the opportunity for use is there should the need arise. Library service can be described as a collective good, in that once it is available to one person, it is equally available to everyone. The other definition of a collective good—that once service is available, it can be provided to others at no added cost—is less applicable to a library. One would need to indicate that there would be some added cost for wider availability although the unit cost would be reduced as the number of users increased.

Society decides how much of its resources to devote to the library and the professional staff is responsible for determining how to allocate resources within the library. As with many professionals, librarians make decisions about allocations on the basis of what they consider provides the best services to the client, and that consumer input to this process is limited. This discussion of who knows what is best for the consumer will doubtless be with us always. Library directors have varied in their approaches: some have developed collections and services to meet a perceived demand for popular reading, others have seen a need to uplift the community through good reading and purposeful services.

COST EFFECTIVENESS

Closely related to the concept of cost-benefit is that of cost effectiveness. Cost-benefit seeks to measure the benefit of a particular activity to the individual, the agency or society at large and to relate it to the actual cost of performing the service. Decisions are then based both on the cost of a service and on its benefits. The manager may well select an option that is not the least costly if it best balances the variables of cost and benefit.

Cost effectiveness is a measure of the extent to which the objectives of library and information services have been met. If, for example, the library manager is concerned about levels of book circulation and the cost of circulation services, a cost effectiveness approach would aim at increasing circulation and reducing unit costs. The cost-benefit approach would have similar objectives but would take into account to a greater degree the attitudes and preferences of clientele and staff concerning the way circulation services are carried out. Cost and effectiveness are objective statements that can be measured; benefit is a subjective statement of value that cannot be exactly quantified.

MODEL BUILDING

Data gathering is often part of the process of developing a model designed to replicate reality. A model is a simple version of a complex reality. Information service and the organizations devised to provide it are exceedingly complex and the design of a model is often helpful in identifying the major components. In the model, major components are identified and secondary variables that may cause confusion are eliminated. In this fashion, the basic aspects of a situation are highlighted and it is easier to understand what is or is not happening. The way in which things fit together can be outlined and the skeleton of the activity plotted. Planners who use models as a means of educating those with whom they are working often use similar models as analogs. For example, the teamwork necessary to win a football game can be a useful way of demonstrating the need for teamwork in an information center, or the costing of the ingredients necessary to making a loaf of bread may be applied to the planning of a line-item or program budget. So long as the analogy is understandable to the audience, it can be a helpful tool.

The model is also a useful framework for the development of a checklist of factors to be considered in decision-making and the types of data needed to make decisions. The factors necessary for decision-making provide a guide to the variables operating within and upon the model. The model itself can be a narrative, or can be in the form of a flowchart or a matrix. Software has been developed which provides a basic planning model and the opportunity to work with a number of variables. These management models are very useful in manipulating variables in many ways and in following the potential results of changing a variable. Care must be taken to assure that the computer-based model selected is appropriate to the situation one is modeling. Whatever model is used, it must show relationships within the model and must reflect the real situation.

COST BEHAVIOR ANALYSIS

It is possible to work toward the development of a cost behavior analysis, which is an attempt to project cost behavior into a future mode for planning purposes—what will be the projected future benefits of a certain activity? Will the development of a CD ROM network for reference services or the opening of a branch in a particular community meet projected needs? What are the likely costs and where will the resources come from? This requires a projection of clientele needs, of income, and of the nature of the service to be provided.

In this type of decision-making activity, a computer-based decision-making model is an asset. One can input current costs and current usage data, project them and gain insight into future relationships between costs and level of usage. Caution is necessary in such an exercise. Trend analysis projects may assume a future with no change in current variables. One learns what probable outcomes will be, given a continuation of current costs of materials, salaries, and present program priorities. If an inflationary figure is built in, it will be an estimated rather than a concrete figure. Despite its drawbacks, however, a computer-based model can be a helpful planning tool in projecting future cost-benefit relationships.

Libraries, like other service activities that are supported by the organization of which they are a part rather than paid directly for the services they perform, have traditionally been managed on past experience rather than on information derived from a study of the operations being performed. "If libraries are to do the best job of managing information in the public interest, then they must know the costs of strategies designed to pass on this information, they must be prepared to identify, measure and control costs, so that the results they want can be afforded and the quantity and quality of information they believe is appropriate to their clientele is available given the financial resources available."[10]

If one receives funding to perform services, accountability naturally follows. To be accountable, it is necessary to know the cost of services. A knowledge of costs is also essential to the planning process, and an informed planning process gives a measure of control over the activities and direction of the library.

A number of activities which are part of the financial planning and budgeting process have been identified here. They are used for analysis of programs as well as in the planning of activities. The purpose of each of these activities is to determine as accurately as possible the costs of programs so that judgments can be made about whether the programs are worth the investment. Whatever the planning budget format, cost determination is the basic building block.

NOTES

1. Stanley M. Altman, "The Dilemma of Data Rich, Information Poor Public Service Organizations: Analyzing Operational Data." *Urban Analysis* 3, 1976, p.61.
2. Douglas Price, "Rational Cost Information: Necessary and Obtainable." *Special Libraries,* 65:2, February, 1974, pp. 49–57.
3. Betty Jo Mitchell, Norman C. Tanis, and Jack Jaffe, *Cost Analysis of Library Functions: A Total System Approach.* Greenwich, Ct.: JAI Press, 1978, p.xi.
4. Ellory Christianson, "Depreciation of Library Collections: A Matter of Interpretation." *Library Administration and Management.* 6:1, Winter, 1992, p.41.
5. Michael Carpenter and Rita Millican, "The Recognition of Depreciation of Library Materials." *Library Administration and Management.* 5:4, Fall, 1991, p.228.
6. Mitchell, et al., *op. cit.*
7. B. T. Stern, "A Cost Benefit Technique for R & D Based Information." Kent, England: The Welcome Foundation Ltd. August, 1970, p.7.
8. Virginia Beach Department of Public Libraries, *Cost/Benefit Analysis of a Catalog System for the Virginia Beach Department of Public Libraries (ED153657).* Virginia Beach, Va.: The Department, 1978, p.5.
9. Robert M. Mason, "A Lower Bound Cost Benefit Model for Information Services." *Information Processing and Management* 14:2, 1978, pp.71–83.
10. Helen Drinan, "Financial Management of On-Line-Services—A How-To Guide." *On-Line* 3:4, October, 1979, pp. 14–21.

V

BUDGET DESIGN

Budgets are classified in a number of ways: by expenditure character, by the user, by who is responsible for preparation, by time span or by some other category. The expenditure character, with which we are concerned here, classifies the document according to whether it is an operating budget, a capital budget, an emergency budget, or some form of extraordinary financial plan. Budgets can also be classified according to the comprehensiveness of their coverage—that is, whether they are general budgets for the entire library, special budgets for departments, or financial plans for special purposes. They can further be differentiated by degree of internal breakdown.

The major distinction is that between expenditures for current operation and those for capital improvements. The former are treated in the present chapter and the latter in the chapter that follows. The general types of operating plans most often discussed are the traditional line-item budget, the program and the performance budget. Zero-based budgeting enjoyed some popularity during the late 1970s but because of the complexity inherent in its preparation, its use has declined and all but disappeared.[1] Despite this, many of the planning elements of zero-based budgeting are useful and for this reason it is discussed here. This breakdown furnishes the outline for the present chapter.

Budgeting, as has been stressed, is a goal-setting activity, a selection of clearly defined ends and of means to achieve those ends. The purpose and function of the budget have changed over the years from a means of control by the funding agency or by the executive to becoming an integral part of the planning process. Formats and systems of budgeting have changed as well, developing from formats with ease of executive control (line-item) to formats with an emphasis on planning and with built-in mechanisms for accountability (program, performance, zero-base, etc.)

BUDGET SCHEDULE

Typically, budgets are prepared for one fiscal year but may be part of a long-term budget planning cycle. The fiscal year for which budgets are prepared varies widely. In designing a budget for a public library, it is not uncommon to plan on the basis of a local government fiscal year beginning January 1, anticipate state funding based on a fiscal year beginning July 1, and federal funding for programs on a year beginning October 1. This variation in beginning dates of fiscal years affects the budgeting activities of all types of information services, although the impact on those that are part of larger organizations is likely to be less than upon agencies such as the public library that are directly dependent on allocations from several government levels. The accounting and reporting cycles are also affected strongly by differences in fiscal years. There must be appropriate reporting to meet deadlines that occur throughout the year.

Most publicly supported agencies operate on an annual budget cycle, with little or no opportunity to carry over funds from one year to another. There is increased pressure in a number of agencies to plan and budget on a long-term cycle. Many programs are long-term and funding them on an annual basis produces uncertainty on the part of those carrying out the programs, as there may be no assurance that funding will continue for the life of a program. With an increasing emphasis on long-range planning, the budgeting aspects of the planning process have become more carefully developed. The long-range budget covering several years may be outlined in a tentative fashion, with annual budgets more carefully developed. Although the long-range budget, like the long-range plan, is subject to review and revision, it does provide a direction and a means of projecting costs for activities that extend beyond the fiscal year.

BUDGET DEFINITION

Budgets are defined by the nature of their expenditures. Operating budgets are annual budgets that outline the cost of operating an agency and its programs for a fiscal year. They include personnel costs, costs of maintaining the physical plant, or purchasing supplies and similar operating costs.

An emergency budget may be necessary in the case of unusual or unforeseen circumstances. If tax revenues have fallen well below anticipated levels or if some other financial crisis has occurred, an emergency budget which reallocates operating expenditures may be required. If there has been a major internal problem, such as fire or water damage which makes the library building inoperable, emergency funds from the funding agency may be provided. Emergency budgeting is usually a one-time activity designed to meet an unexpected critical need. If it is not in response to fiscal crises, it is in addition to the operating budget and the two are kept separate but used in parallel by the administrator.

Budgets can also be defined by the sources of revenue. In most not-for-profit services, funding comes from tax revenues or contributions from citizens. These vary according to the level of government and whether the funds are general purpose or for a special purpose. Contributions vary from membership fees to bequests or other gifts.

Budgets differ in comprehensiveness. The general or overall budget covers the operating costs of the entire library. There also may be special-purpose budgets to meet specific needs. Departments will have their own budgets which are subsets of the general budget. Reference service, technical services, extension services, etc. usually have their own budgets. There are also budgets designed to meet the requirements of a federal or state grant or similar special project. Bequests may be part of the library's income and if they provide special-purpose funds, they may require separate budgeting and accounting.

Budgets can be defined according to the expenditure classifications that were emphasized in discussion of the planning process. They may be program-oriented, with goals and objectives as the basis of the planning process, or means-oriented with goals assumed or unexamined.

BUDGET FORMATS

Budgets are also differentiated in more general terms as to whether they are traditional line-item documents or program or performance, or whether they follow elements of the zero-based format. This classification serves as the basis of this and the following chapters. Each type of budget has been used or considered for use by library managers. Each has benefits and difficulties in implementation. Each is related to the other in certain respects and, to a degree, the newer budget formats have been built upon and are adaptations of earlier forms. Elements of one format are often incorporated into other formats.

The format selected by a library is in large measure a reflection of what was done the previous year or what is being done by other agencies of the institution or government. If other libraries are reviewing and using newer budget formats or if there is local pressure to change, the library may consider changing its format. If there is no pressure and if the library manager is not particularly enthusiastic about change, more traditional formats are likely to be followed. There is almost always one constituency that prefers the status quo and another desirous of change.

In budgeting for the 1990s the major consideration is to provide the services expected by various constituencies in an environment of reduced financial resources. In the continuous improvement environment, library customers expect to be involved in determining the ways in which services are provided, and in some cases *which* services are provided. They often want additional services or augmented services despite the reduction in financial resources. As library customers become sophisticated in the use of the electronic highway, their expectations rise further.

Inflation reduces the value of the dollar and the ability of the library to maintain an existing level of service. Increased taxes or higher prices tend to anger the constituencies paying for the service. Citizens expect good service but in many cases will not or cannot provide the dollars that will insure adequate service. One is in a position similar to that which caused Louis Brownlow in 1933 to comment that ". . . one tries to look into the future and see what is ahead for cities. He can hardly fail to see that the immediate task . . . is that of making buckle and tongue meet."[2]

Budgeting consists of three broad activities: planning, allocating and reporting. Much of the emphasis in earlier chapters has been in the planning function; later chapters will emphasize the reporting function. The emphasis here is on the allocation function as it reflects the planning process that has gone on before. Four major budget formats—line-item, program, performance, and zero-base—will be emphasized, the latter more as an example of the relationship among planning, budgeting and accountability than as a format that is currently in use. Other formats such as lump sum and formula-based budgets will be mentioned briefly but are not as widely used or as useful.

LINE-ITEM BUDGET

The line-item or object of expenditure budget is the most common form and has been used for many years. Based entirely on line-item accounting, it lists those items necessary to conduct an activity, such as personnel, equipment, supplies, and books, usually in a standard format that does not vary from year to year or from agency to agency. Continuity is thus provided and the new budget can be constructed from the previous year's document by listing the same line items and by varying amounts to be spent depending upon recent experience. Little planning is necessary in developing this type of budget, as cost figures can simply be increased to meet inflationary factors.

If careful accounts are kept, the spending picture for each item indicates the extent to which the budgeted amount for that item was appropriate. An item for telephone costs might be well under budget because of the installation of a new system, while the utility costs may be well over the allocated amount because of unusually cold weather. Adjustments to reflect changed expenditures in certain items plus an inflationary factor constitute the new budget proposal.

This type of budget is closely related to incremental budgeting under which whatever is in the budget is to an extent frozen and the new budget is developed based on increments to the base figures. These types of budget—line-item and its incremental variation—are easy to prepare as they are based on previous action, and are easy to control in that variations in each line item for the agency can be plotted and reviewed over a number of years. It is possible to determine the extent to which salaries or the supplies necessary to run a library have increased. The relative cost of one agency can be compared to that of running other similar agencies within the overall governance structure, or to the cost of running a similar activity in other universities, urban governments or industries. Budget development and accounting are both simple, following a standard form and practice.

The major problem in line-item budgeting, and it is a fundamental problem, is that there is no requirement for planning. The budget can be developed independently of what occurs in the library. It

Activity No.	Department: Library	Division:	Section: Sub.	Fund: General	

Acct. No.	Classification	Actual Expenditure 1980	Actual Expenditure 1981	Budgeted Expenditure 1982	Department Request 1983	Recommended by Manager 1983	Final Budget 1983
	PERSONAL SERVICES:						
11-01	Salaries						
011	- Full Time	$145,724	$177,224	$227,537	$245,737	$245,730	
012	- Temporary				9,406	9,400	
013	- Part Time						
014	- Overtime						
015	- Sick Pay						
11-02	Social Security	8,566	10,400	14,260	14,799	14,800	
11-03	Pension	7,241	8,690	12,100	12,274	12,270	
11-04	Hospitalization	5,765	6,331	9,540	9,594	9,600	
11-05	Life Insurance	486	493	730	790	790	
11-06	Longevity	2,564	3,144	3,520	4,052	4,050	
11-07	Workmen's Compensation Ins.	-	-	70	514	520	
11-09	Payroll Contingency						
	TOTAL	$170,346	$206,282	$267,757	$297,166	$297,160	
	SUPPLIES:						
12-01	Office	$ 3,970	$ 4,197	$ 5,900	$ 9,341	$ 9,340	
12-02	Operating	44,069	55,948	113,828	113,828	93,830	
12-03	Repair & Maintenance	1,897	3,493	5,480	7,296	7,300	
	TOTAL	$ 49,936	$ 63,638	$125,208	$130,465	$110,470	
	OTHER SERVICES AND CHARGES						
13-01	Professional Services	$ 5,488	$ 2,936	$ 8,060	$ 8,060	$ 8,060	
13-02	Communications	-	2,603	3,830			
021	- Postage	2,089	-	-	1,664	1,670	
022	- Telephone & Telegraph				2,888	2,890	
13-03	Transportation	-	7,380	-			
031	- Travel & Training	7,508	-	990	250	250	
032	- Equipment Rental	-	-	7,000	6,941	6,940	
13-04	Advertising						
13-05	Printing & Binding						
13-06	Insurance	1,462	1,765	2,620	5,280	5,280	
13-07	Public Utility Service	7,233	7,322	14,900	18,601	18,600	
13-08	Repair & Maintenance	2,777	2,921	3,740	4,604	4,600	
13-09	Rental	1,554	1,853	3,200	3,514	3,520	
13-41	Miscellaneous	70	100	130	130	130	
13-42	Judgments & Losses						
13-43	Aid to Other Gov. & Agency						
13-51							
	TOTAL	$ 28,181	$ 26,880	$ 44,470	$ 51,932	$ 51,940	
	CAPITAL OUTLAY:						
20-02	Equipment	$ 3,901	$ 2,724	$ 1,100	$ 1,071	$ 1,070	
20-04	Land						
20-05	Buildings						
20-06	Improve. other than Bldgs.						
	TOTAL	$ 3,901	$ 2,724	$ 1,100	$ 1,071	$ 1,070	
	GRAND TOTAL	$252,364	$299,524	$438,535	$480,634	$460,640	

Figure 1 Line-Item Budget

would be an extreme case to have a line-item budget prepared with no consideration of library activities, but it is possible. Line items identify the ingredients of a program, but not the product. Books, work stations, staff and space are funded rather than, for example, reference service. The service must conform to the budget dollars allocated for its various ingredients. A planned program places emphasis on what is done or will be done, and *then* the resources needed to carry out the plan are itemized. In the line-item format, a set of resources is identified and the task is to put them together as best one can to form a program.

PROGRAM AND PERFORMANCE BUDGET

Program budgeting and performance budgeting seem to be interchangeable terms, depending on which authority one cites. This is particularly evident when one tries to follow writings on library applications of the two.

Program budgeting was first recommended by the Hoover Commission in the late 1940s and was adopted by the federal government in 1949. Performance budgeting came along a decade or more later. Young[3] asserts that performance budgeting and program budgeting are not interchangeable terms but reflect different budget approaches. The United Way of America Service Identification System (UWASIS) defines the two as being interchangeable. This conflict in definition causes difficulty when one attempts to describe or explain these systems.

According to Young, "Program budgeting emphasizes the services that have been developed and assesses the dollar allocations in serving the needs of the clientele. Program budgeting usually requires the presentation of alternative ways of providing necessary services at different funding and priority levels."[4] He describes performance budgeting as "activity budgeting" that is efficiency-oriented and places emphasis on the work to be done and its unit cost; examples would include providing a film service, providing service to a nursing home, or circulating books to users. Here the program budget will be defined in accordance with the earlier UWASIS view of it as program- or function-oriented; this in fact reflects Young's definition of a performance budget. The performance according to some other definitions is output-oriented and assesses the success of dollar allocations.

It was this concern for what is done rather than the resources for doing it, this change in emphasis, that served as the catalyst in the development of budgeting systems based on planning. In the twentieth century there has been a steady move on the part of governing bodies toward planning for services rather than simply reacting to existing crises and deciding how to use available resources to meet them. The past four decades have been a period of increasing professionalization in the ways in which institutions, both public and private, have gone about using resources to meet people needs. The key has been planning; planning ways to best utilize resources. Planning encompasses a wide variety of activities, one of which is budgeting.

The planning process, as we have seen, is based on a series of steps that include:

1) an agreement on the broad goals or mission of the institution
2) selection of specific objectives from a variety of possible objectives
3) gathering and analysis of data in order to determine appropriate objectives
4) selection of the most appropriate means of achieving the objectives
5) development in detail of the way in which the objectives are to be achieved. This is the programming step and the point at which specifics are turned into budget items.

Program planning precedes the development of a program budget. In the planning stage, specific objectives are established and the activities the information service is responsible for carrying out are selected. The budgeting activity is the placing of dollar figures next to the programs. What the agency is to do has been determined. The next step is to determine the cost of the programs to be funded.

This form of budgeting has a number of names—functional budgeting, performance budgeting, or program budgeting. It is based on the concept of functional accounting, which requires that agencies report their financial activities in terms of the programs and services they provide rather than in terms of line items. Within each function a line-item reporting system is then used. This was recommended in 1949 by the Hoover Commission as a means of focusing attention on the work to be done by various agencies. The

Commission gave the name performance budgeting to what had formerly been called budgeting by function. It also used another term—program budgeting—to denote similar activity. "Performance budgeting is management oriented: its principal thrust is to help administrators to assess the work efficiency of operating units by (1) casting the budget in functional terms, and (2) providing work cost measurements to facilitate the efficient performance of prescribed activities."[5]

Although budgets are contracted for a year's expenditures, the activities of the funded agency are ongoing and the planning for the agency is on a long-term basis. The current year's budget is part of a continuum of long-term planning. That planning takes place within the context of the mission and goals of the agency and is implemented through the methodology of program analysis. Hatry and others have described this methodology as consisting of eight steps:

1) define the problem
2) identify relevant objectives
3) select evaluation criteria
4) specify client groups
5) identify alternatives
6) estimate costs of each alternative
7) determine effectiveness of each alternative
8) present findings.[6]

The major issue in the planning process is the effective allocation of resources. The above systems-analysis approach provides a means of clarifying objectives in a quantitative fashion rather than basing them on experience or on unsupported assumptions.

The budget cycle of planning, preparation, submission, approval, execution and audit is part of the overall planning cycle. That the annual sequence is part of a long-range planning cycle becomes particularly apparent as one develops program budgeting systems where ongoing and long-term programs as well as short-term ones are part of the process. The current budget plan is to an extent the result of decisions made in earlier budget years. Long-range planning is useful in helping to insure that those earlier decisions were and are sound.

The budget is developed by departments within a library and in time becomes a single integrated budget. If there is competition among departments for funding, each departmental program may be developed, not as part of the overall budget, but as a program statement of one unit designed to compete with other units. This creates or has the potential for creating a politicized environment in which competition for dollars may be more active than program integrity. Strong, centralized managerial control is necessary to integrate departmental programs and resource requests into an overall program. "If program budgeting and systems analysis are to be done effectively, the bureaucrats in the lower echelons of government who have day to day responsibility for the operation of specific programs must have some self interest in the application of these techniques."[7]

Program budgeting in its planning mode requires involvement by trustees, administrators and staff. The development of community analysis and planning guides have provided us tools which place emphasis on the user and ways in which the library's clientele can be represented in the planning/budgeting process. An early tool was *The Planning Process,* published in 1980 by the Public Library Association of the American Library Association.[8] It has been followed by a series of tools and guides to assist in bringing together library planning and customer expectations. The development of total quality management techniques has also provided tools to assist in the process of assuring that the services provided mesh with consumer wants. From these tools and techniques, both basic planning data and priorities for service as expressed by various constituencies can be retrieved.

The library's objectives come from a meshing of community needs by the funding agency. These may be in some conflict and negotiation is often necessary to identify those information needs that will be met. Once the objectives and services of the information agency are agreed upon, a long-range plan can be put in place to meet them. At the same time that this is being done, it is necessary to determine the resources that are and probably will be available to carry out the objectives. Budgeting, by definition, is the allocation of scarce resources to the carrying out of objectives.

The next step in the planning process after objectives have been established and resources identified is to collect data to support the program that emerges. For any program, there will be personnel costs, costs of material and supplies, overhead costs, etc. In this budget format those costs are grouped around the program or function. For example, let us assume that the reference department has agreed that it will provide an on-line search service to small business. Staff would collect all cost figures for the program. The first and most expensive cost is that of personnel. This will include the salary of the individual during the time they are negotiating questions, conducting the actual search, sharpening their searching skills, or engaging in any other activity directly related to the searching activity. If supervision or training is required, the cost of the amount of time spent will also be calculated. If clerical support is needed this too will be added to the cost according to time spent. As direct salary costs are only about two-thirds of the actual cost of staff, benefits must be added in at the appropriate rate for each level of employee. The total of these factors will be the actual personnel costs. Cost of work station purchase or lease and the cost of thesauri or other search supports are included, as is the cost of paper for printouts and the cost of any additional supplies required to conduct the task. The cost per square foot of space used to house the activity is included as well. Overhead costs, which include the cost of heating, cleaning and insuring the space used, plus the administrative costs of managing the overall library service, may be included for each program or may be called an administrative program, with all such costs identified together rather than being broken down for each program.

If the decision by the library administration is to absorb the cost of searches, then the cost of connect time and data base use would also have to be included in the program. A figure for the cost of an average search would be calculated and the number of searches in a particular time frame would be estimated. This calculation would not be necessary if the direct cost of the searching is passed on to the user; only if it becomes library policy to subsidize the service in whole or part.

The program resulting from the data collection for on-line searching might look as follows:

Department: Reference

Program: On-line search service

Description: To provide in-depth on-line bibliographic search service to small business.

Anticipated accomplishments: To provide small business enterprises with quality searches at reasonable cost.

Workload Indicators: Use statistics to be maintained.

Positions:
   Professional
   Non-professional
   Benefits

Equipment
   Work stations
   Printers
   Thesauri

Supplies: List of all forms, paper and other consumable supplies needed to perform search services.

Contractual:
   Rental or lease of equipment
   Costs of data base use
   Telephone communication

If the overhead costs are broken out into a separate program, it is not necessary to list them here. From the above collection of data for this program, a cost figure will be derived. Other examples of such financial development are given in Figure 2.

All of the data, except for those needed to determine the amount of staff time devoted to the program, should be available in the library's existing records. They will need to be rearranged from a line-item format. Supply costs can be allocated from the general supply line item to individual programs according to their use in each. In order to obtain the data on staff time allocated to each program, a time study will need to be made. In its simplest form, this is a record kept by each staff member indicating all the activities they perform during a stated time period; appropriate amounts of their time can then be allocated to specific program activities. A methodology for time studies is available in the management literature and is fairly easy to follow. The major difficulty is that the time necessary to conduct the study is apt to be resented by staff members who are asked to record their activities. A further difficulty is that staff may see the exercise not as an objective time study but as a way of checking to see whether they are working enough.

Administration

> Personal Services
>> Salaries
>> Personal Benefits
>> Training and Conferences
>
> Interdepartmental Services
>> Auditing
>> Insurance
>> Automobile Expenses
>> Building and Grounds Maintenance
>> Printing and Reproduction
>
> Contractual Services
>> Rental of Space
>> Telephone
>> Utilities
>> Equipment Rental
>> Maintenance Service
>> Membership and Dues
>
> Supplies and Materials
>> Office Supplies
>> Postage
>> Maintenance Supplies
>> Janitorial Supplies

TOTAL ADMINISTRATION

Circulation Services (Sample Narrative)

Description: Record all loan transactions; maintain circulation and registration records; generate required statistics; keep collection, card catalog, and other collection access tools in order.

Anticipated Accomplishments: Convert charging system to a new automated format.

Figure 2 The Program Budget[9]

Workload Indicators: Annual circulation statistics for three prior years, and a projection for budget year based on the past year's experience.

Positions
  Professional
  Nonprofessional
  Clerical
  Benefits

Equipment
  Charging Equipment
  Card Catalog Unit
  Book Truck

Supplies
  Listing of all paper, forms, record-keeping supplies to circulation service

Contractual
  Rental of Copy Machine
  Printing
  Binding
  Collection Rentals

Similar descriptions, anticipated accomplishments, workload indicators and resources will be listed for each of the following:

Reference Services
Children's Services
Audiovisual Services
Bookmobile
Outreach
Branches
Special Services (e.g., federal grant to be administered which would be recorded here with grant funding to be reported under income)

TOTAL

Figure 2 (continued)

Administration

Personal Services
   Salaries
   Personal Benefits
   Training and Conferences

Interdepartmental Services
   Auditing
   Insurance
   Automobile Expenses
   Building and Grounds Maintenance
   Printing and Duplicating

Contractural Services
   Rental of Space
   Telephone
   Utilities
   Equipment Rental
   Maintenance Service
   Membership and Dues

Supplies and Materials
   Office Supplies
   Postage
   Maintenance Supplies
   Janitorial Supplies

TOTAL ADMINISTRATION

Figure 3 Operating Budget Performance Budget Format[10]

Input Cost	Service	Program Objective	Output Totals	Cost Per Output
$84,430	General Service	Provide library materials and equipment	187,650	$ .45
63,570	Circulation Service	Lend materials to public	298,460	.21
35,280	Reference Service	Provide readers advisory and reference service	33,601	1.05
36,000	Bookmobile Service	Provide circulation and services to patrons in Green and Stone counties	4 bookmobiles	9,000.00
6,960	Outreach Service	Provide materials for physically handicapped and institutionalized	12 stations	580.00
14,640	Records Service	Maintain records of use and users for statistical reports and planning input, overdues sent, etc.	11,340 persons	1.29
15,860	Special Services	SDI, special research projects to individuals or groups	463 services	34.26
1,300	Public Relations Service	Publicize library resources and programs	104 programs	12.50

Once a program budget is in place, usually replacing the line-item format, there will have been a major change in the planning/budgeting scheme. The emphasis has been shifted from "what do you need to provide information service, people, materials, space?" to "what is the purpose of information service, what are its goals and objectives, and what programs are necessary to meet those goals?" Only after those inquiries are answered does the question of what is necessary to meet objectives arise. Resources are scarce and must be allocated with care. Allocating them according to a plan of programs to be implemented places the emphasis on what is done rather than on the inputs necessary to get the job done. In this format there is accountability both in terms of fiscal responsibility and in the extent to which program objectives are achieved. Politically, the move toward this second kind of accountability can provide strong support for library programs. Those who were never sure what a library was about can gain some insight. The other side of the coin is that once the funding agencies are made aware of the cost of certain programs, they may decide that they are too costly and recommend their elimination.

Programs should be subject to continuous review to permit adjustment to meet changing conditions. Regardless of the governance structure within which the library is located, in the overall program format it is a program labeled LIBRARY. Within the university structure that program competes with instruction, research, and housing. Within local government it competes with health services, social services and emergency services; and in the industrial environment it is often part of the research program, the public information program or some other larger activity. The format that the library's budget takes is determined by that of the larger governance structure and must be in conformity with it.

A further refinement of the program budgeting system is PPBS, the Planning Programming Budgeting System or Performance Budgeting. It builds on the same techniques and philosophy as the program budget but carries it a step further to include an evaluative element. Where the program budget identifies goals and programs to carry them out, the performance budget includes a measurement factor to respond to the question, "How are we doing—are we meeting our objectives and to what extent?"

Much of the literature and review of program budgeting and performance budgeting has combined the two in such a way that it is often difficult to distinguish one from the other. In fact, the latter is a continuation of an existing system rather than a completely new system. Its emphasis is on the determination of the purpose of a library or other institution, a clarification of its objectives, and the development of programs to carry out the objectives. In PPBS there is a greater emphasis on measures of program effectiveness and the opportunity for decision-making based on the extent to which programs are meeting objectives. According to Young,[11] PPBS facilitates decisions because of the analytical data bearing on objectives that it generates. He emphasizes that purely economic factors are not sufficient for decision-making, that social and political inputs are also essential.

The emphasis of PPBS is on planning to meet objectives, and it is in the planning steps that the greatest amount of change and new learning will take place. Conclusions can be reached as to what priorities actually exist and changes then made if that is desirable. Choices are next made as to which of a number of alternative methods is best for implementing the agreed priorities. To carry this out there is need for a decision-analysis unit—a person or group competent to review data and provide cost figures for programs and alternatives.

Principal types of output indicators are: number of items circulated, people registered as borrowers, individuals attending a program, and similar data. These can be collected for varying time spans depending on the availability of data and the planning needs. Some activities are not quantifiable and there is no point in trying to force quantification. This is particularly true in the case of the many service-related functions of an information center. The number of reference questions answered is no measure of quality or of user satisfaction. It should be remembered that volume indicators serve as a guide to how much the library is doing rather than how well it is doing. They do provide a guide to the size of clientele and help to allocate resources in response to use. Sudden changes in volume indicators also help to alert planners to areas requiring attention.

When selecting output indicators, it is important that they meet certain criteria:

1) The measure selected should be directly relevant to the program for which it is used. Circulation data are inappropriate as a measure for reference service and on-line user measures are appropriate only to one facet of reference service.

2) Select the fewest and the simplest measures which will describe

the program adequately. For bookmobile use, no more than circulation and number of patrons served may be necessary. The number of miles traveled, age of patrons, and other interesting data are less informative and, although they may be useful for other purposes, are not the best measure of the program. The measures should be easy to collect and readily available. They serve to measure a program already in place and are used to monitor its performance. Although it would be managerially convenient to have measures for every activity, quantifiable and easy to produce, this is often not the case.

These program data feed into the long-term plan for the entire institution, broken down by administrative and service units. The plan will have been devised based on the purpose of the library, the environment within which it is located, the clientele it serves, and the resources available to provide services. Early versions of the plan reflect what the current level of service is, and development of it gradually encompasses change in clientele and in direction to reflect changing need. Although in theory a plan should derive from needs alone and provide the best means of meeting goals and objectives for the benefit of clients, in reality the planning process is tied to resources and moves at the rate at which resources become available. In many instances program-oriented budgeting may exist side by side with other budgeting systems as managers work their way from one system to another.

The early versions of the program plan will be based on the best estimates of the departments providing service. To assure the most useful, albeit still rough planning data, projected expenditures should reflect the present and projected size of the inflation factor. Comparable levels of service should be the basis of all estimates. Some generally agreed upon decisions will help to provide comparability of data among the various departments of the library. The initial plan is comprised of the best set of decisions for the next year and has a tentative quality. As data are collected on performance, decisions will be modified.

Actually two plans come into place—the program plan and the financial plan. Although they may cover the same time span, the program plan will include a number of long-range projections that go beyond the time span of the financial plan. The program plan includes current and long-term objectives; the financial plan emphasizes current operations to a greater degree. Both have to be regularly reviewed and updated, based on changes in purpose, in activities and in resources.

Indicators of output provide an ongoing performance measure. They are not in themselves an evaluation but serve as a monitor to alert the decision-makers to areas needing attention. The plan is a guide and the indicators show how the plan is implemented.

Most agencies dependent upon public monies are tied to annual financial budgets. They may have to plan resource allocations on an annual basis. However, the purposes of the agency are usually long-term and ongoing. Long-range plans which, within the context of the legal authority and responsibility of the agency, direct the way in which that agency carries out its responsibility are necessary. The major asset of a planning system tied to budgeting is that there is a link between plans and resources and this is set with a long-range time frame. Earlier line-item formats emphasized the short-term aspects of funding and although the manager may have had a general long-range direction for the library in mind, it was not formalized and often was a personal rather than an institutional plan.

ZERO-BASE PLANNING

A decade after the arrival of the performance budget, a variation and extension of budgeting and planning appeared. Zero-base budgeting was first heralded in print in a 1970 article by Peter Phyrr which appeared in the *Harvard Business Review*. The first implementation of a system that could be called zero-base was in 1964 at the U.S. Department of Agriculture. By the end of the 1970s a number of state governments and private industries had experimented with it, with varying degrees of enthusiasm and success.

"Zero-base budgeting (ZBB) is a planning and budgeting process that involves decision making at all levels of management, starting with a zero base for budgeting and justifying the entire budget request in detail. It requires that all programs and operations at all levels be identified in decision packages, evaluated, and ranked in priority order."[12] It starts from the belief that every enterprise must periodically justify its existence. The concept of zero-base budgeting is of an operating, planning, and budgeting process that requires each manager to justify every request for budget funds in detail; the burden is on the manager to prove the need for funds.

The general steps in this system, as in program budgeting, begin with the clarification of organizational goals and objectives, and proceed to a careful examination of the existing structure, functions and activities. Decision units are identified. These are subdivisions of the organization which have responsibility for implementing particular allocations. They may include department heads, a program director, or other officers or subdivisions. Once the decision units have been identified, decision packages are prepared. A decision package is a statement of objectives, current operations, alternative actions, and possible funding levels of a unit. The decision packages are reviewed and ranked and, from this, an overall budget is prepared.

Those who advocate the system aver that it results in greater efficiency, better management, and wiser use of financial resources. Those who are not advocates point to the complexity and time-consuming aspects of the process. As with many innovations, it has often been oversold and poorly applied, and is usually not well understood. It is a complex system, not one to be learned quickly and not one to be applied without the advice and consultation of someone comfortable with the process. Although a survey of academic budgeting activity conducted in 1992 showed zero-base budgeting to be among those least often used,[13] the elements of the process continue to be useful tools for planning and budgeting.

In looking at planning and spending in the zero-base way, one uses many of the same tools of cost accounting and performance measurement that are used in other budgeting systems. The planning aspects of this system are extended and expanded beyond those of other systems. Zero-base budgeting places emphasis on projected results: what is to be accomplished, at what level, and the way in which it is to be accomplished. Before dealing with these questions, the primary question is whether the activity should be conducted at all; whether it has lost its importance to the organization or whether it is still viable. In theory, in justifying expenditures managers will sort out those programs that no longer merit high priority, and these will receive reduced or zero funding. In practice, few programs have so little support that they can be easily eliminated.

The zero-base technique is highly evaluative because, in addition to justifying the existence of a program, one must also justify the level at which it should be funded and gauge the results to be anticipated from the agreed-upon funding level. The manager determines objectives for each organizational entity and establishes operational and then expenditure guidelines. To do this requires an evaluation of operations, proposed courses of action for achieving objectives, cost and results of expenditures at several levels of funding as well as recommended priorities for activities. Top management reviews the managers' reports, revises priorities to bring them into line with overall objectives and allocates resources accordingly. Once questions concerning the purpose of a library or information service, its objectives and the directions the service will take have been answered, planning and funding decisions will follow.

The first step in zero-base budgeting is to examine the current budget structure and define each budget unit. In a sense, this is an organization chart built along lines of responsibility for spending money. It will, to a large degree, conform to the standard organization chart, but there may be some variations. Once this is done, each service increment is defined and analyzed. This is the smallest possible unit of service and includes such things as the operation of a public library branch, a current awareness service for researchers, or a series of film programs. It is a basic assumption that even if an activity merits funding, it can be funded at a level below the current level, and the service less than the current level can be offered. The question is then asked, "What levels of service are technically feasible?" Beginning with the lowest possible provision of service, several levels are identified. The lowest level of service is the survival level, where only the most important activities at the lowest possible levels are provided.

In the case of the operation of a branch library, this might mean that the branch would be open only ten hours per week for circulation of materials in and out. No reference services or program activity would be available. The next higher level would add increments to the service and each addition would require justification in terms of its contribution to the achievement of organizational goals. In the case of the branch library, this might include the addition of hours of service, some new materials for circulation, and the availability of professional staff for reference services during part of the hours open.

Normally two or three levels of services are identified, each with added benefits justified in terms of the extent to which those benefits meet organizational objectives. Present levels of service are usually described at the third level of service. A level of service about the present would be the optimum level for achieving the objectives of the organization. Each level of service from survival to current and to optimal includes a description of activities and added costs. The decision-maker then selects the level for funding.

Each service within the library is identified and analyzed in the above manner. The managers of each budget unit meet to discuss the relative merits of each service and its increments. The services are then prioritized. Typically there will be more demands for funds than funds available. The general manager funds the service increments in order of agreed priorities until all funds are allocated. This process is carried out within and among departments throughout the institution.

If the objective is to allocate funds rationally within an organization by prioritizing programs and service levels, this is a useful technique. The result can be a generally agreed-upon set of funding decisions, justified in cost/benefit terms, and accompanied by performance measures for each decision package. To reach this result takes planning, negotiation, and considerable effort.

Additional benefits accrue as management analyzes current practice and plans for future activity. The close review of each activity will reveal differences that may exist between practice and the directives of the funding agency. A large and complex organization may be meeting its responsibilities at different levels in different parts of the organization. In addition, standardized formats and a fixed format for presenting budget information provide the manager with comparable information from various units.

In an organization in which planning and budgeting have been limited to a few individuals, the inclusion of line managers in the decision-making process may be stressful to those accustomed to more central control. Department heads and others responsible for programs are the ones who make initial decisions regarding levels of service and funding. Zero-base budgeting "is one means of involving lower management in decision making processes, of fostering initiative and of winning commitment."[14] Zero-base budgeting is more than a budget system. It is a management improvement strategy that eventually leads the organization to management by objectives, to long-range planning for programs and resource allocation and to tying inputs to outcomes.

Managers should be aware of potential drawbacks before becoming involved in zero-base budgeting techniques. It is a time-consuming activity. Because of the potential it has for realigning the decision-making process, it must receive full support of the board or other governing body. It is a complex process and is best developed with the help of guidelines and consultation with individuals who are experienced in working with it. As the process proceeds, employees may see the decision-making activities, particularly those that reduce current levels of service, as dangerous to their own livelihood and may resent the process. This method does not eliminate political considerations and interpersonal rivalry—indeed, it may intensify them. Although improved communication is often cited as a benefit of the process, the result can be a glut of paperwork which can hinder communication. After studying and experimenting with this system, one official indicated that he would recommend it only if the current budget system did not generate appropriate information. He stressed that this is no sure route to achieving budget reduction and re-emphasized its complexity.[15] Although there have been more than two decades of experimentation with the zero-base process, most of the writing on the subject deals with how to do it rather than reporting experience in its implementation. Those articles reporting experience tend to applaud the planning process and the decision-making elements, but caution that the amount of time and effort necessary to implement the process may seem excessive.

The implication of the term zero-base is that if a program's existence cannot be justified within the mission and goals of the organization, it has zero justification for funding. In this way, non-relevant programs would cease to exist. Not surprisingly, managers can usually justify the existence and expansion of their own programs.

For those who wish to investigate the process, the following provides a general guide to implementation. The first specific step is to identify decision units within the institution. These are discrete activities that can be identified and analyzed. The organization chart of the library is a hierarchy of decision units, with each small unit part of a larger one, and so on up through the lines of authority. A decision unit may be a project such as the development of bibliographies, a service such as circulation of materials, or the activities of a group such as reference service. It always has a measurable output resulting from budget allocation and can be related to a function of library service. The decision units and those responsible for ranking their importance are the basis of the implementation structure.

Each activity must be described by a decision package which includes:

1) Objective, purpose and scope
2) What is to be done and how

3) Consequences of not doing the activity
4) Alternative methods
5) Alternative levels
6) Costs and benefits of recommended alternative methods and levels
7) Resources required[16]

The package can be costed out at different levels of effort and with different benefits and consequences. The manager determines the level at which funding should take place.

Once all decision packages are prepared, they are then ranked in order of priority, in terms of their importance to the carrying out of overall objectives. This is done initially at the department level, and then all packages and departmental rankings are passed on to the higher administration for review and re-ranking in light of institutional objectives. Those ranking highest will be funded; those at lower rankings may be eliminated. In a non-political environment such a system has a chance of working, but problems of interpersonal and departmental rivalry often emerge in the ranking process. This has been recognized by those devising the system but no ready solutions are apparent.

There are a number of similarities between program and performance budgeting and zero-base budgeting. The former has never been particularly popular as it often assumed that there was one best way and level of achieving objectives. The zero-base approach has greater flexibility. The major difference between program budgeting and ZBB is in time. Program/performance is a long-range budgetary management system with the emphasis on planning. An environment is developed within which techniques such as cost-benefit analysis and systems analysis can be used. ZBB is a short-term technique within the planning context. Decisions are required concerning each program on an annual basis. In program/performance budgeting, the overall program is reviewed, but not each year and not with an overt decision to fund or not to fund.

By the 1990s zero-base budgeting had come to be seen as a collection of useful tools that can be applied to planning, prioritizing, investigating and reviewing operations. Although zero-base budgeting as a total process was officially abandoned by the federal government in 1981, and although of a number of the corporations using it some abandoned it, elements of the process have been retained and are seen as useful tools.

Figure 4 Zero-Base Budget

DECISION UNIT SUMMARY

DECISION UNIT NAME: Interlibrary Loan

1. OBJECTIVE OF DECISION UNIT:

To manage interlibrary loan service so that all faculty, staff, graduate and undergraduate students receive satisfactory service, in terms of locating requested items and providing shortest possible delivery time.

2. CURRENT OPERATIONS AND DESIRED RESOURCES:

There is a head of interlibrary loan, two searchers, three clerks and student help equivalent to one full time subprofessional position.

3. LIST ALTERNATIVE WAYS WHICH COULD ACCOMPLISH OBJECTIVE AND REASON FOR NOT USING IN 1982.

   a. Purchase all items requested for loan--limited acquisition budget, limited potential use of many requested items, delay caused by ordering materials usually greater than delay in borrowing.

   b. Issue universal borrowing cards to borrowers so that they can visit holding institution and use items there--limited number of potential holding institutions in area.

4. SUMMARY OF INCREMENTS FOR 1982. SERVICE PROVIDED

(Identify the "Current" Level):	Increment Number	Incremental		Cumulative		Work-loan/ Performance Summary			
						Quality		Quantity	
		Expense	Employees	Expense	Employees	Customer complaints (per month)	Delay in order processing (days)	# ILL	New ILL (cum.)
Head of ILL, 2 Searchers, 1 Clerk, 5 FTE Students	1 of 4	53,620	4.5	53,260	4.5	9	8	4,000	600
Add 2 clerks	2 of 4	17,000	2	69,360	6.5	7	10	5,000	1,100
Add .5 Students FTE	3 of 4	3,120	.5	72,480	7	5	3	5,000	1,100
Add 1 Searcher	4 of 4	12,000	1	84,480	8	3	3	5,400	1,400
	of								
	of								
1981 Forecast expense and employees				55,600	5	5	3	4,400	900

Sample Ranking Table

(1) Organizational Units being ranked Library		(2) Prepared by W. Prentice	(3) Date 6/9/80	(4) Page 1 of 1
(5) Decision Unit Increments		(6) 1981 Proposed	(7) 1981 Cumula- tive	(8) 1980 Forecast	(9) % Change 1981 - 1980 x 100
Rank	Increment Number	Expense	Expense	Expense	Expense
1. Interlibrary Loan	1 of 4	53, 260	53, 260	55, 600	
2. Online Searching	1 of 3	25, 000	78, 260	31, 600	
3. Bibliographic Instr.	1 of 3	42, 100	120, 360	49, 300	
4. Interlibrary Loan	2 of 4	17, 000	137, 360		
5. On Line Searching	2 of 3	16, 000	153, 360		
6. Interlibrary Loan	3 of 4	3, 120	156, 480		
7. Bibliographic Instr.	2 of 3	13, 400	169, 880		
8. On Line Searching	3 of 3	9, 500	179, 380		
9. Interlibrary Loan	4 of 4	12, 000	191, 380		
10. Bibliographic Instr.	3 of 3	6, 240	197, 620		
	of				
	of				
	of				
	of				
	of				
Total		197, 620	197, 620	136, 500	

OTHER BUDGET FORMATS

Formula budgeting has been applied to academic institutions. Although its reception has been mixed, a number of states adopted this technique as a part of the funding process for publicly supported institutions. Formula budgeting assumes that levels of funding can be calculated on the basis of number of students, size and level of academic programs and the level of publication of educational materials. The concern for the development of formulas for funding is strongest at the state level. More than a decade ago, it was apparent that "there is a trend toward statewide systems of academic libraries with co-orientated funding, planning and coordinated programs. . . . This trend is growing because of declining budgets, rising costs and space shortages. . . . Budgeting authorities are more willing to provide increased library funding . . . if a statewide academic library development has been articulated and approved."[17]

A number of funding formulas have been devised. Perhaps the best known is the Clapp-Jordan formula developed in the mid-1960s and based on what the opening day basic collection should be. Using number of faculty, number of students, number of undergraduate major subject fields, number of master's fields and number of Ph.D. fields, a review of basic lists and subject bibliographies, plus professional experience and judgment, it was assumed that a *minimal* level of adequacy could be determined. This was not a budgeting formula and was not intended as such, but it has been used by some states and institutions for this purpose.[18]

The Washington State formula, used in the early 1970s and then phased out, is a modification of Clapp-Jordan and is in turn based on the plan devised for but not used by the University of California. The University System of Florida uses a formula based on the Washington model. This formula is based on existing book and journal resources, and staffing and binding. A currency factor (5%) to maintain an overall updated collection is used instead of reviewing titles for each field. An allowance for new program fields, a replacement factor, and an organized research factor are the criteria on which the formula is based. The total of the units of resources to be added in a fiscal year are converted into dollars using a standard dollar value per unit except for base-year periodical and serial commitments.[19] Library operations factors, including FTE (Full Time Equivalent) students at four levels of instruction, total FTE faculty, maintenance of current collections, acquisition, and basic staffing assumptions, are calculated. Binding is calculated on the basis of the number of current subscriptions, assumed to equal one binding year, plus a rebinding factor. The formula became too complex and in the state of Washington there was concern over the accuracy of library data and over the level and treatment of the currency issue. Other states, including Texas and North Carolina, designed formulas for funding but either did not use them or used elements of the formula.

Variations of formula funding have used calculations for levels of instruction, subject emphasis, and enrollment factors. Some are simple, but others, like the Washington Formula, die from their own complexity. After a trend toward ever more complex formulas, there has been a recognition in some areas that the formulas are too complex to be useful. Whatever formulas are used, they are rarely fully funded because of economic and political pressure. While academic libraries in the state university system of Florida are funded by formula, allocations are usually at a percentage of full funding. Efforts to vary the formula to take into consideration the different needs of mature university libraries and the libraries of the newer universities further complicate formula-based funding as it is applied in Florida.

Other budgeting formats, which in reality are not formats but an absence of form, are grouped around the general term "lump sum." This is at the opposite end of the spectrum from any planning approach. The library is given a sum of money and told to function on that amount of money for a period of time. Such a method can indicate primitive funding principles or a lack of interest in the library and its purpose. If the library director is alert, this can become an opportunity for the library to develop its own planning format and allocate the lump sum to program objectives. Except in poorly run situations, de jure lump-sum budgeting is rare. It is less rare to impose a pro forma budget system, usually of the line-item variety, and then allocate a sum of money having little to do with the budget request: this results in a form of de facto lump-sum budgeting.

Each of the budget systems described here has differing levels of planning implications and each has economic and political implications as well. The one implemented by the individual library will depend largely upon decisions taken by the parent institution or government. Which format to follow is rarely a decision made by the library manager. Knowing the benefits and difficulties of the major budgeting systems is essential for managers, however. It may be possible to test aspects of program budgeting or devise zero-base decision packages as a way of reviewing aspects of the library program.

Despite several decades of discussion about budget formats and many recommendations for change, most libraries still follow a line-item format. A small but increasing number are adapting formats which emphasize the functions and programs of a library and allocate funds accordingly. The requirement of performance budgeting—that measures of performance or output be identified—serves as a block to widespread acceptance of this approach, in large part because of the difficulty of devising generally acceptable performance measures for a service which is performed in a not-for-profit setting. As public demand for accountability increases, performance measures are being tested and incorporated into the planning budgeting cycle. Zero-base budgeting, after a flurry of experimentation in the mid-1970s, is now used as a source of planning techniques but is regarded as too unwieldy to be used as a full budgeting system.

We are now able to look at a range of budgeting techniques, compare them, take pieces from one or the other and adapt them to specific needs. However simple or complex the system, the purpose is still to allocate scarce resources to meet stated objectives. When resources are most scarce, the tendency of political authorities is to opt for the simplest budget format. For the library planner, the lesson would seen to be that internal planning can be complex and detailed and the internal budget decision-making process carefully structured, but the end product that emerges for external consideration must be simple and easy to understand in its larger implications and should not appear too different from what the funding agency expects.

NOTES

1. Harry Hatry, "The Alphabet Soup Approach: You'll Love It." *The Public Manager* 21:4, Winter, 1992–93, p. 9.
2. Louis Brownlow, *Municipal Yearbook.* Chicago: International City Managers' Association, 1934, p. 3.
3. Harold C. Young, *Planning, Programming, Budgeting Systems in Academic Libraries.* Detroit: Gale Research, 1974, p. 9.
4. *Ibid.*, p. 9.

5. United Way of America, *Accounting and Financial Reporting*. Alexandria, Va: United Way of America, 1974, p. 71.
6. Harry Hatry, et al. *Program Analysis for State and Local Governments*. Washington, D.C.: Urban Institute, 1976, p. 4.
7. Jack Ochs, *Public Finance*. New York: Harper and Row, 1974, p. 99.
8. Vernon E. Palmour, *A Planning Process for Public Libraries*. Chicago: American Library Association, 1980.
9. Ann E. Prentice, *Public Library Finance*. Chicago: American Library Association, 1977, pp. 97–98.
10. *Ibid,* pp. 102–103.
11. Harold C. Young, *Planning, Programming, Budgeting Systems in Academic Libraries*. Detroit: Gale Research, 1974, p. 5.
12. Gary E. Kindey and Earline P. Taylor, "The Financial Officer's Toolbox." *NACUBO Business Officer* 27:11, May ,1994, p. 30.
13. *Ibid.*, p. 30.
14. Richard K. Taulbee, "The CPA in Industry," *The Ohio CPA Journal* 48:4, Winter, 1989, p. 53.
15. *Ibid.*, p. 53.
16. *Ibid.*, p. 54.
17. Isaac T. Littleton, *State Systems of Higher Education and Libraries: A Report for the Council on Library Resources*. Raleigh, N.C.: The State University, November 1977, p. 31.
18. Verner W. Clapp and Robert Jordan, "Quantitative Criteria for Adequacy of Academic Library Collections," *College and Research Libraries* 26:3, September 1965, p. 371–80.
19. Littleton, *State Systems of Higher Education and Libraries,* p. 57.

VI

CAPITAL BUDGETING

The operating budget which was discussed in the preceding chapter focuses on the development of an orderly means of funding ongoing activities for a stated period of time, usually a year. Recurring expenditures such as salary, utilities and supplies are itemized in some way in order to assure that the program of activity is supported.

The capital budget is a separate budget developed in coordination with the operating budget, but its purpose is different, as is its planning cycle. The capital budget, and the capital program of which it is a part, can be viewed as a multi-year operating budget which deals with those programs which cannot be accomplished within a year and/or which are high-cost, single-purpose programs. Their purpose is to assist in accomplishing specific long-term operating goals. A library is built to meet the goal of expanded service, networked computer work stations are purchased to provide more efficient service, or a branch library is built to meet the needs of extended service. Although the capital budget may be perceived as separate and different from the operating budget, it is, in its most important aspect—the planning aspect—an extension of the long-term operating budget. Both are developed to achieve the same underlying goal of improved information service and are highly linked.[1]

CHARACTERISTICS OF THE CAPITAL BUDGET

Planners have listed those special characteristics of the capital budget which make it different from the operating budget.

1) The capital budget supports a distinct, major activity, such as the construction of a new building, the renovation of an existing building or the purchase of a new computer system. Because of the

impact of such an activity, there is a long-range anticipated effect on the staff and on the community served and to be served.

2) In developing the capital budget, it is recommended that the anticipated lifetime of the building or computer system or whatever major activity is the focus of the plan be taken into account. For example, for a new building there is a twenty-year span before major renovation is needed. The capital budget must be long-term in the reality of the projected cost of the building.

3) It must also build in the expectation that acquiring sufficient funds to start construction is a time-consuming effort, sometimes taking five or more years.

4) A new library affects the community served in a number of ways. Capital budget planning must take into account the overall environmental impact of a new building. In an academic setting, the location will be determined in part by available suitable land and by the location of other libraries within the institution. It will also be affected by the attitude of the academic community toward the role of the library in the learning process. Is it central or peripheral? And should the library be located in the center of the academic community or to one side? Library location also affects traffic patterns, parking needs and the overall configuration of the campus. Many colleges and universities have developed a master plan for the growth and development of their campus, taking into account the above variables and adding an appreciation for the aesthetics of location and style of projected buildings as well as for overall functionality within the academic setting.

Planning for a public library building is subject to similar considerations. They may be more directly expressed through the decisions and regulations of planning and zoning commissions. Any capital project that will have a long-term impact on the community served must be reviewed in the planning stage by those who are responsible for the overall plan and design of the community— usually a city planner or agency responsible for the master plan. Regardless of the type of information agency for which a new building, a new section of a building, or major refurbishing is projected, these or similar considerations will apply and will have budgetary implications.

5) The capital budget is not limited to one fiscal year. It has been called a multi-year operating budget focused on a single program in order to provide an orderly progression in carrying out that program over an extended period of time.

6) One of the difficulties with a capital budget is that it can be postponed indefinitely, as it is not usually tied to a deadline. If the state or municipality is funding a capital project, the funds are subject to availability from revenue sources or bonds. If the economy is ailing, expenditures are reduced to meet income. Deferring capital projects from one year to another is a standard means of keeping budgets in balance. During periods of financial difficulty, capital expenditures are often limited. If expenditures are deferred too long, the physical plant of the academic institution, the public buildings of a city, or the home of a specialized information service can drop below desirable levels, requiring additional expenditures. If the capital budget is dependent upon fund-raising activities by the library and its supporters, the project becomes open-ended in terms of time, and actual implementation of the program may not begin until sufficient funds are available.

7) In a small community, a capital expenditure is likely to affect resource allocation for some time. Large capital expenditures occur regularly and many communities plan a percentage of their income to be used for capital improvement. In this way there is a regularly budgeted cost rather than a large expense in any one period of time.

City, university or other planners may prefer that capital expenditure proposals originate with agencies providing service, so that need is established by those most familiar with the program. Agencies will then need to compete for funds. The planner or planning agency becomes the mediator among agencies and in this fashion asserts overall control. Another means is for the city, university or other group to use its master plan for development as a means of scheduling in new buildings according to anticipated need as determined by this larger group. Political considerations play a major role in determining which projects are looked upon favorably at any particular time.[2] Still another view of capital expenditure is that of trustees, alumni, local business interests and similar groups who see it as a means of enhancing the economic well-being of the community. For example, a fine new library is an asset to the community it serves and will attract new users and additional traffic.

DEVELOPMENT OF THE CAPITAL PLAN

The development of a capital plan by an agency is a necessary step in acquiring funds to carry out a project, regardless of the source of those funds. If a public library intends to seek funds through private foundations and local industry as well as public monies, the plan and budget serve as a means of estimating both need and the means required to meet that need. If a library intends to request federal funding, either directly or through the state, such a plan is the first step. In one sense, the capital budget can be considered as a program budget in support of a specific objective.

Most states have legislation covering the ways in which a publicly supported institution can go about the process of developing a capital budget. Privately supported institutions and corporations are not subject to such regulations unless they plan to request public monies. Whatever the governance of the group developing a capital budget, it is wise to investigate the legislation related to the activity.

The process begins with the establishing by the institution that a major capital outlay is necessary if the institution is to meet its responsibility to provide adequate service. This justification is reached as a result of the same planning process and data inputs as are used for the operating budget, for the two in the end have the same goal. The inputs include current and projected levels of service, current and projected resources, and space needed to house those resources, as well as reviews of the changes in services and resources which occur as a result of technological advances, demographic changes, or other long-term trends. Initial planning should be done by library staff with whatever consultation is deemed necessary. The planning report should be carefully prepared so that when it is presented to those less familiar with library and information needs, it will provide sufficient background in a form that is convincing and acceptable to governing authorities and to the public.

ESTIMATION OF CAPITAL EXPENDITURE

Once the plan is developed, an estimate of the capital expenditure is prepared. This estimating process involves a number of steps, the first being a justification of the proposed capital improvement as the appropriate means of meeting the program objectives of the institution. If the proposed capital improvement is the building of a new public library branch, can the program be justified on the basis of anticipated increased service, the extent of existing use, and demographic projections for the area? Would the rental of an existing building, the extension of bookmobile service, or some other alternative meet the stated need as well and at less cost? Costing out the various alternatives and determining their relative benefits is an important early step. Once the decision is made that a new branch library is the appropriate means of meeting the program objective, additional program choices are made in the same fashion. Alternatives are identified and costed out. Location of the branch is one such decision. Real estate cost varies with location and availability. Research indicates that the library is used more heavily when it is central to community activities, and is easy to reach by foot or car. Economy may dictate placing the branch on the periphery of the community to be served. Available sites are identified and the possibly conflicting factors of access by the user and cost of land are negotiated. Further planning considerations include the type of library to be constructed. Is it to be a low-cost structure or will it be more elaborate? What type of design best meets the objective of the building's use? At this point architectural consultation is essential.

Once these and related questions have been answered, a cost estimate is possible. Cost figures are presented in current dollars and will vary in the future with the rate of inflation. Today's projected cost for a branch library will be honored by architect and builders for a limited time only. As the time span for the capital budget can be open-ended, the estimates will need to be revised regularly in response to increasing costs. When estimates are made at the library level, they will typically reflect the cost of the best possible branch library to carry out the program. When they are reviewed at a higher level, compromises are probable and the resulting estimate may eliminate items that cannot be justified as essential. Materials and fees may be reduced as the review process continues and such reductions will be reflected in the quality of the new building and the care with which it is constructed.

OBTAINING FUNDING

Developing a capital program and a capital budget is the first step in obtaining funding. Obtaining the funds, a more difficult step, is a political activity strongly affected by prevailing economic conditions. In the case of a public library, there is the additional factor of social and cultural conscience, which may have considerably less to do with the ultimate delivery of information than with the community's feeling that it shows a lack of social concern not to fund a library. Experience has shown repeatedly that when the choice is between safety (police and fire protection) and information, or when funds are limited, social and cultural conscience lose out. An added factor is that more people are employed by local government in health and safety-related jobs than in information positions; they therefore exert more influence on decision-making.

The decision to fund construction of a branch library is an economic one and the community must have the financial resources to make the investment. During a recession, as tax collection on sales tends to decrease and the cost of unemployment payments and related human service costs are higher, it may not be a wise decision, economically or politically, to fund a new branch library construction project unless it can be shown to provide needed jobs.

BOND ISSUES

An important means of funding capital improvements by tax-supported institutions is through the borrowing of money, and an understanding of how this process works is important. The library board and/or chief administrator would typically submit a request to the local government for a bond issue to fund a major capital improvement. If approved by government officials, the request would then be placed on the ballot, usually at a regular election, and the voters would decide whether or not to approve the request. In most states a simple majority assures passage.

Before submitting a proposal for voter approval, the library staff and supporters should plan carefully. Except in the case of an emergency, such as a fire that destroys the existing structure, there is time to plan, and planning for voter support is just as important as planning for a building or other proposed capital expenditure. It is axiomatic that good service is the best advertisement for support of library service. But there is also a need to publicize the service, so that all taxpayers, not just regular library users, are aware of its benefits. Continuing service needs also require constructive publicity, emphasizing the improved service that is possible with added resources.

Municipal debt is incurred by local governments in anticipation of revenue. It is a loan on future income and should be incurred only for capital expenditure. Money is obtained through the sale of municipal bonds. More than 100,000 counties, cities, towns, authorities and special districts in the United States issue bonds for short-term or long-term needs. There are a number of types of municipal bonds, the most common being a full faith and credit general obligation bond. With this kind of long-term debt the issuing agency's credit is fully pledged against its principal asset—the agency's tax income. State law regulates this form of borrowing closely. The non-guaranteed debt, a second type of long-term debt, is payable from the earnings of revenue-producing activities. Since libraries produce very little revenue, they are rarely considered for this type of funding. Because there is no assurance that revenue will be sufficient to pay the debt, bonding consultants do not guarantee these loans. Other types of bonds include lease rental bonds issued by a non-profit organization that puts up the money for capital improvement and then charges rent over a period of time until the debt is retired. This type of arrangement can be made with a private as well as a public agency.

The procedures for preparing and presenting a bond issue are part of state law and are designed to assure that no local government unit borrows beyond its ability to pay interest and to repay capital. In the nineteenth century there were instances of municipalities which had borrowed for capital improvements and then defaulted on their loans when tax revenues fell below expectations. The municipality's ability to pay is based on its tax income, and during a recession that income may fall below anticipated expenditures. State legislators have therefore placed strict limitations on the bonded indebtedness a municipality may incur.

Not only has the state restricted indebtedness; it also determines tax structures. The municipality thus has limited control over its sources of income to pay for development. In addition to state legislation controlling taxing power, referenda recently passed by voters in several states have reduced the right of government to tax above a certain level. Since these referenda are usually directed at reductions in the property tax, it is local government that is hardest hit. Under these circumstances less and less local money becomes available for operating budgets and there is likely to be less and less opportunity for bond issue success.

If the voters approve a bond issue and the municipality is legally able to borrow, the final step is to find someone willing to buy the bonds. Each municipality has a credit rating based on its economic health, its fiscal management patterns, its record of repayment of debts, and its level of current indebtedness. The rule of thumb is that overall debt should not exceed ten percent of assessed valuation. Ratings are done nationally and are reported in *Moody's Investor's Service* by Standard and Poor. Bonds may be purchased by brokers who buy and sell securities, by municipal bond departments of banks, or by brokers who specialize in certain types of bonds. Most municipal bonds are sold at public sale to investment brokers at a price that insures a fair profit. If a municipality accepts the bid of the prospective buyer, the bid becomes a contract to purchase the bonds. The bonds are then sold by the brokers to customers, and as they are a non-taxable form of investment, municipal bonds have a particular advantage to the investor. The bond market is not attractive if interest rates are increasing, because the resale value of the issues declines; the reverse is true, of course, if interest rates are going down.

Only after the sale of bonds is money available for capital expenditure. The process is long and involved and difficulties can occur at each step. Before starting down this road the library should have its own long-term plan—one that meshes with the plans of the municipality. The success of the library in this type of financial activity is dependent upon both careful planning and the way in which these plans are shared with the community. Politics plays a strong role on the library's success, and economics an even greater role. When there is sufficient money in local coffers the library does well, but when money is less available the library is one of the first to feel the pinch.

Communities, like families, have a desired life style, a level of income and priorities for spending it. Poor communities, with an insufficient tax base, live hand to mouth, paying first for fire and police protection, health and welfare costs, and street maintenance, and only after these needs are met do they look at education and information. More affluent communities have a greater measure of choice in deciding how to spend their tax dollars.

When needs arise that cannot be met by the annual budgeting for library service, the relationship of the library to the community is put to a test. A major campaign of informing the community of library needs is obviously called for, but the success or failure of a bond issue vote is usually determined by the attitude toward libraries and library service built up over a long period of responding to community information needs.

At the time of a bond issue, the role of groups in informing the community of library services and needs is not to be underestimated. Friends of the Library have organized in many areas and serve as a link between the library and the community in a way that governing bodies, such as trustees, do not. The two serve differing important functions; trustees are responsible for policy and governance, Friends for keeping the library before the public and to help provide support for library programs. Friends typically belong to other community service groups and widen the range of community awareness of library service in an effective fashion, thus building support for library bond issues.

OTHER FUNDING OPTIONS

If a public library plans to fund the construction completely or in part through contributions, a number of financing possibilities are available, depending on the structure of library governance and local legal restrictions. If the library is a quasi-independent body, as in the case of an association library, it may borrow money and plan its own payback system. The new building and whatever other assets the library holds would be used as collateral. A similar situation applies with independent educational institutions, associations, and other similar groups. A more common means of funding is to set up a capital reserve fund to which contributed funds are added until the total is sufficient to finance the proposed expenditure. These funds could be invested in high-interest-yield notes for the specified periods. If the cost of construction appears to be rising rapidly, it might be prudent to contract for construction at once and borrow money to supplement the reserve fund.

Once a building has been constructed, many library administrators adopt a pay-as-you-go method for finishing and furnishing the building. This provides for an earlier construction completion date, but may greatly extend the time before which the building is usable. The advantage of the pay-as-you-go method is that there are no interest payments on loans and each addition is paid for immediately. The disadvantage, in addition to the lengthening of the completion period, is that inflation costs can nullify the interest savings.

USE OF FUNDS

The capital budget, once the expenditures begin, is typically used for the acquisition of land, payment of professional fees, and other contract awards. Each of these activities is governed by state law or local regulation. The project is monitored as it progresses to insure quality of workmanship and adherence to cost agreements. This process is usually part of the contractual agreement with the architect or project manager, but municipalities or educational governing bodies may have their own project reviewer on site to safeguard the interests of the purchaser.

Throughout the capital planning and expenditure process, the plan and budget are subject to review in the same way as any long-range plans. Until contracts are signed and other commitments made, revisions in the plan are possible. Because a capital investment is easily identifiable, the success of its completion and implementation is obvious. Equally obvious will be any major errors that occur and, unfortunately, errors remain longer in the memory than success. For this reason, if for no other, capital planning and budgeting should be conducted carefully, and revised thoroughly before commitments or expenditures are made.

For services like library service that meet general needs not tied to a specific municipality or agency, there have been some moves toward cooperative capital planning and budgeting. Combined school-public libraries are one instance of this. Another instance is the combined college-public library, such as that built cooperatively by Unity College and the town of Unity, Maine. Libraries built to serve more than one association or group of professions are possible, as are academic libraries built to serve more than one academic institution; an example of the latter is the Auraria Libraries in Denver, Colorado, a single library serving four academic institutions. Public library needs in adjoining communities might well be served by joint planning by the two communities for a new building to serve both. Combining a senior citizen or community center with a branch library has been done in Tampa, Florida and in Carroll County, Maryland. Problems of governance and control are present in each of these options, and if enhanced service is to result from cooperative action, compromises may be necessary. As costs of construction and of library service increase, some form of cooperation may become a necessity.

CAPITAL BUDGETING FOR OTHER
THAN BUILDING PROGRAMS

Capital budgeting is not applied solely to buildings. It can be used for the purchase of a number of long-term non-consumable items. Bookmobiles and other vehicles, furnishings, computer equipment, both hardware and software, as well as major collection purchases can be acquired through a capital budget. If such acquisitions can be made through the operating budget, this is usually the preferred method, but there are instances where expenditures may exceed the capacity of the operating budget. A substantial outlay in computer equipment and networking support is often beyond the capacity of the operating budget to absorb. Usually the rule is that if the purchase exceeds a certain dollar amount, if its useful life is three years or more, and if the expense is non-recurring, it may qualify as a capital budget expenditure. Although computing equipment is often obsolete after three years, an initial outlay which will bring the organization up to a desired level of information access and manipulation would be a candidate for capital funding, perhaps with the expectation that upgrades and maintenance would appear in the annual operating budget.

Sometimes collection development activities can come under the capital budgeting umbrella. Some libraries have considered purchasing periodicals on a three-year subscription basis rather than on an annual basis. The price of the multi-year subscription is lower than the annual rate and there are lower handling costs. Renewals do not need to be made as often and the longer subscription period protects the buyer from possible rate increases. The difficulty is that few libraries have sufficient funds to enter into multi-year subscriptions from an annual acquisitions budget. For those institutions that are allowed to purchase services in advance of delivery, this can be a capital budgeting opportunity in that it concerns the purchase of items that will not be consumed within a short period and the costs are multi-year in nature. A decision, once made, would be very difficult to reverse and " . . . because each alternative has multiple year streams of costs and benefits associated with it, the cost of capital to the institution is an important variable in the decision.[3] The criterion for decision-making is the relationship between cost minimization and a constant quality acquisitions policy. Questions requiring response include the cost of borrowing money to purchase serials on a three-year basis as related to the cost savings of the longer subscription period. The library would save in re-order costs as well as in the cost of rate increases. A disadvantage is that marginal serials, which would otherwise be ordered for one year as a test, would have to be ordered for three years.

A model was devised for one study, interrelating the various factors to determine which of three alternative methods of serials acquisitions—continuation of annual subscription purchase, immediate change-over to the purchase of all subscriptions on a three-year basis, or a phased change to three-year subscription purchase—was least costly. The time span selected was six years. Twenty periodicals were used as a sample and their predicted inflation rate estimated through the use of linear regression analysis. Estimates of staff time required for renewals were made. The findings of the study indicated "that more resources be expended immediately in serial acquisition in order to spend less time in the long run."[4]

This is an example of an adoption in the non-profit sector of a hedge against inflation commonly practiced in the for-profit sector. If inflation continues, and presumably it will do so for some time, it is more cost-effective to borrow money and purchase at today's prices than to buy as cash becomes available. Because of the way in which tax-supported institutions are funded, this option may be difficult to pursue and may well be legally prohibited in some cases. For the library in a governance structure that is not tax-supported—such as the private university, the association library, or the library in a for-profit enterprise—capital budgeting of large equipment purchases, collection development or other major non-consumables is a technique to consider. This method may also improve service by making resources available at once rather than at a future date. Buy now and pay later is often good planning in an era of inflation.

Capital budgeting is an important means of funding major objectives of the library. In a period of inflation it may take on added benefits as a means of providing buildings or equipment today at prices which are probably lower than they will be in future years. Careful use of this type of budgeting in tandem with the operating budget provides the overall budgeting system for the library.

NOTES

1. John P. Forrester, "Municipal Capital Budgeting: An Examination." *Public Budgeting and Finance* 13:2 Summer, 1993, p.92.
2. *Ibid.*, p.86.
3. Guilbert C. Hertschke and Ellen Kehoe, "Serial Acquisition as a Capital Budgeting Program." *Journal of the American Society for Information Science,* September, 1980, p.357.
4. *Ibid.*, p.358.

VII

SOURCES OF INCOME

The income with which a library or information agency funds its activities is derived from a number of sources; these vary with the governance structure within which the information service operates and whether it is a for-profit or not-for-profit organization. The public library, the public academic institution, the public school, and publicly supported specialized collections such as a county crime laboratory collection or a public museum's collection are funded largely through tax dollars from state and/or local sources. The private educational institution is funded by a mixture of tuition income, investment income, and public money. Societies such as the American Institute of Physics and private groups such as the supporters of the Morgan Library in New York City or those supporting the photography collection and resources at the George Eastman House in Rochester, N.Y. derive their support from private donations, investments, or contributions from members. The specialized information resource within a for-profit environment is usually listed within the administrative budget and is funded in a manner similar to other aspects of the company's operation. Library systems, networks and cooperatives are funded under a variety of arrangements, typically with a mix of state and federal funding. Added to these sources of income are categorical and non-categorical aid from the federal government to groups providing information. This particular source of income changes in terms of amounts available in response to federal funding priorities. Private sources of income from foundations, from industry and from individuals constitute an additional resource, as do organized fund-raising and fees charged for service. Fees for services, which may be for cost recovery or may be intended to serve as an additional revenue stream, have become increasingly prevalent as on-line data bases and other costly means of information access are available to the users.

INCOME AS RELATED TO GOVERNANCE STRUCTURE

In discussing major funding patterns, it is appropriate to group them by the major types of governmental or business settings within which they are found. The public library, as a department of local government, is the information service most directly involved in the funding process. The public academic institution budget includes the library, but, within that structure, funding decisions are made that serve as an additional level of income justification between library and funding source. Similar levels of decision-making are interposed between information agency and funding decisions in most other not-for-profit institutional situations, such as schools and museums. The information agency budget in business, industry or other for-profit setting is usually part of the administrative overhead of the organization and its funding is negotiated as part of the larger package.

The public library is largely supported by the tax dollar and the largest percentage of that tax dollar derives from the local tax base. In the past decade, the percentage of public library support received from the tax dollar has decreased from a high of from 85 to 90 per cent to an average of 77 per cent in 1991, and the expectation is that the percentage may well drop further.[1] Despite discussions about state funding and regional funding possibilities, the library is still firmly set in the local funding environment. The policies affecting the sources of income and the uses of that income are a product of historical, economic, environmental, and cultural forces, each of which makes demands on the political system. "State and local decision makers are dependent upon the economic forces within their jurisdiction, forces over which they have relatively little control"[2] If sufficient economic resources are not available to fund the level of public services expected by the community, difficulties arise. This has been the situation for some time in most jurisdictions, due in part to the decreasing relative value of the property tax in the community, the impact of inflation, and the resistance by taxpayers to increases in their taxes. Numerous local tax revolts have resulted in a capping or a reduction in property taxes, further reducing the availability of dollars to support local service.

In any taxing system the rewards and benefits are unequal. Some individuals will contribute more than others and get less in return. Each form of taxation—property, sales, income—imposes its burden in a different fashion and affects various groups differently. Each object of expenditure—be it education, highway maintenance, police protection, health care, etc.—offers different rewards to different groups. Library and information service is one of the few publicly funded services that offers equal rewards to all groups, although not all segments of the community take equal advantage of the offer. Its public nature crosses economic levels. Because it benefits all it is often taken for granted, and because it is a general good it seldom has the partisan or group support of a more controversial service to special interests.

Within any community, there are conflicting views among different interest groups about the appropriate way to spend tax dollars. When there are sufficient funds, conflict is reduced, but conflict increases as funds become more limited. In any publicly funded budget a large percentage of the expenditures is mandated by law or local regulation. Allocation of the remaining funds is subject to a combination of local custom and pressures from local interest groups and elected officials. Decisions on the allocation of those funds that are not used to meet mandated costs are made not as much on the basis of objective, noncontroversial measures as they are the result of the conflicting influences of beliefs, bias and fuzzy truth. Those who make appropriations will never satisfy all interested groups. Some of those involved in the decisions have the interests of the community at heart; others are self-seeking.

Although the focus of the decision-making process is allocation of money, more is involved. For the library, general support by community groups and elected officials is equally important. Promises and goodwill do not pay salaries or buy materials, but they can and must be nurtured so that the climate for future dollar increases is favorable.

Local government officers have greater difficulty in solving financial problems than do those in the federal government, as there is very little local control over the economy and there are rigid restrictions preventing indebtedness and limiting tax-rate increases. Local and state agencies are often required to implement funding decisions made for them at the federal level. If there is a decrease in local funds because of reduced revenues, federally mandated program funding is not reduced; in fact, it may increase, as when unemployment and welfare costs increase in a time of economic recession. In addition to federal mandating of funding levels, other income may be earmarked for special purposes; for example, the allocation of the gas tax to highway maintenance.

Added to limitations in freedom over funding choices and in decision-making powers, local and state officials who make decisions often have limited expertise. Although state and local freedom in financial decisions is limited, these restrictions serve as a protection against undue expenditures beyond present or projected ability to pay.

To a considerable extent libraries in the public sector have been associated with education, and have often received attention, both good and bad, similar to that received by education. Public libraries and public schools have been lumped together by some people when discussing funding principles. This becomes important in the planning/funding process because of the political powers that are invoked. In some states, school districts have direct taxing powers. Schools may have special access to funds not available to other local agencies. They are responsible for meeting state-mandated require-ments and many have part of their budget provided by the state. This special category is becoming more and more populated by other agencies as part of their funding is provided from the state or federal level.

This gradual taking over of the funding of local activities is encouraged on the one hand by local officials because it helps meet local needs without large local tax increases. It is resented on the other hand because, as local funding is reduced, local control is reduced as well. The gradual process of moving local government control away from local officers will doubtless continue, and resent-ment of this loss of control will grow. The national debate over more government or less government is intense, and despite political statements that support less government control, the reality is that local control will continue to erode. One of the indications of this is the presence of federally mandated programs which are to be financed locally.

Schools, as a major investment, traditionally held onto as a major area of local policy-making, are further along the road toward control at a higher level; hence the growing resentment against many school policies. Public libraries are also affected by increased state and federal influence and although the amount of money expended on them is less, and therefore resentment is less, they too receive a share of negative local thinking. The library profession stresses the need to increase state and federal aid for funding libraries at a reasonable level. The question that remains is whether the financial benefits are partially offset by outside requirements and by political resentment over loss of local control.

The tax levied for library services is limited in certain states to a specific millage rate; in others no rate is specified. In addition, most legislation dealing with the funding of public library service is enabling legislation. Communities, if they wish, can establish library service, and once that service meets certain governance and other requirements, it qualifies as a recipient of tax dollars. There is no requirement that a community must have a library and that it must be funded. In a sense, libraries are funded out of the beneficence of local officials rather than because they are a mandated element of local government.

INCOME AS RELATED TO ECONOMIC FACTORS

The availability of dollars to support local services is dependent upon economic growth, an increase in real income per capita. This occurs when government, business, and individuals opt to invest rather than to use their resources. A conflict arises here between the desire to increase the ability to generate future income through basic research and capital investment and the desire to meet present social and educational needs. Is health care for the poor or educational enrichment of the learning-disadvantaged more or less important than the building of an industrial park to attract new business?

The availability of tax dollars is also dependent on economic stability, a condition of high employment and constant productivity. There are conflicting theories as to the effect of increased or decreased tax rates on inflation. Economists and government officials have tinkered with these variables for over a decade, with little apparent success. Inflation has continued, economic growth has slowed, and the most significant result has been a loss of faith in government among those who are governed. This has had its most overt manifestation in various taxpayer revolts.

Localities at one time or another find themselves in stressful situations economically. The closing of military bases as the cold war wound down, and layoffs in many companies of all sizes as they re-engineer their operations, provide examples of the problems that can be created at the local level as a result of international and/or national pressures. Services traditionally funded by local government are not fundable at previous levels just at the time when the need is most urgent. In this situation, state or federal assistance in funding can help maintain an adequate level of support despite local economic stress. When the stress is widespread, as during a recession, little or no assistance from other levels of government can be expected.

For a time during the 1980s the federal government experimented with "supply side economics," which focused on stimulating private investment and economic growth rather than on government manipulation of the economy. During the 1980s taxes were cut and regulations eased. While some parts of the economy prospered, the overall result was that federal deficits soared and by the end of the decade the economy was in recession. We now live in a world in which the local, state, federal and world economies are intertwined and in which the difficulties or benefits in one area affect other areas. The economic health of a community is only partially under the control of the community and its leaders must be attuned to the larger environment.

The economist is interested in allocation of scarce resources. The manager is interested in the use of resources once they have been allocated. The political scientist is concerned with the political impacts of the allocation of resources. Each of these views is important in shaping the final decisions as to how resources are used, and each must be explored as local financial policy is developed.

These economic factors lead to several conditions that determine the ability of local government to finance services:

- the number of revenue sources available and the relative emphasis placed on each—property tax, sales tax, state and federal sources, etc.
- decisions on capital improvements, whether funded from revenues or through bonds
- patterns of indebtedness
- the freedom local government has to vary its fiscal policies dependent on changes in the economy.

TAXES AS A SOURCE OF INCOME

The resources which are used to support public library service are part of the income of the local government authority under which the library is established. The library may be chartered to serve a city, a town, a county, a school district or a special district. Depending upon state laws and local regulations, it qualified for a share of the tax support of local government. The taxes are received by local government largely from the property tax and to a lesser degree from local sales and income taxes. Within a special district, a special library levy may be voted.

The major resource has historically been the property tax. Until the mid-1920s this was the most important source of revenue for government in general. It was a stable resource and taxes were relatively easy to collect. The property tax as a source of revenue declined rapidly after 1927. By 1963, when compared to all tax revenue collected at all levels on a nationwide basis, the property tax generated less than half the general revenue and less than a third of state revenue. The prediction that the property tax as a source of income would continue to decline as a part of local income has been borne out. In 1978–1979 only 56 per cent of the total municipal tax revenue came from the property tax.

Local government officials, attempting to stabilize the property tax as a source of income, raised the assessed valuation of property in many areas, thus allowing them to collect additional revenue. While property taxes are easier to administer than other taxes and the amount can be predicted accurately, they have several shortcomings. Property taxes are regressive and place a heavy burden on those less able to pay, those on fixed incomes, and those whose homes are their major investment. Uneven assessment practices can further complicate the fair allocation of taxes. Such factors account for growing taxpayer resistance to the property tax. Because of the difficulty many retired homeowners have in paying increased taxes, they have become a strong voting group and are influential in opposing budget increases and bond issues. They have supported referenda to limit the extent to which property taxes can be levied and have in some instances forced a roll-back of existing property tax rates. Other states, observing taxpayer revolts, have placed limitations on expenditures as a means of forestalling such votes.

A further limitation on excessively high property taxes is that business and industry will tend to settle and stay where the tax situation is most favorable to them. The balance between assessing at adequate levels and incurring taxpayer wrath over high rates is a difficult one. In an inflationary economy, it is not possible to generate enough increased income from property to offset increasing costs without an adverse reaction.

The property tax, because it is so entwined in state and local law, will continue for some time to be a major source of local income. Because of the near impossibility of raising it substantially, two options are open to a local government; to reduce tax-supported services radically or to try to increase other sources of local revenue. Communities continue to insist on high levels of service and the impact of a reduced standard of community living has gradually become apparent to the taxpayer. Roads in poor repair take longer to be fixed, health services are less comprehensive, class size in the schools is larger and the library patron has increasing difficulty in locating more recent materials. So long as reduced taxes result in layoffs, many taxpayers seem to be satisfied that local government is headed toward a leaner model. But when the physical plant deteriorates and services decline, the impact of sharply reduced spending may affect them differently. Admittedly, local government has developed inefficiencies in some areas and planning has not been consistent, but the cut-backs will do more than force efficiencies.

A second option of local government is to seek additional sources of tax revenue. The source of government revenues has shifted in the past half-century from the property tax to the income tax. This is a normal transition as one moves from a society based on agriculture and the land to one based on industrial growth and the ability of the worker to earn a salary rather than derive a living from the land itself. The difficulty for local government is that it is third in line to benefit from income taxes. The largest part of the income tax is taken by the federal government. Most states also impose a state income tax. Those local governments that tax income can claim only a modest amount.

The advantage of the income tax is that it is progressive, claiming a greater tax from those with higher incomes. It is also easy to collect, in that it is taken from workers' paychecks as a required deduction. Its disadvantage lies in the resistance by the worker to being taxed a third time on earned income. Local income taxes also serve as a deterrent to the growth of local industry since prospective employers prefer to locate in areas more favorable to their employees.

A third source of local revenue is the sales tax. Although universally disliked, by the merchant who must collect it on each taxable purchase and by the customer who is constantly reminded of being taxed, this regressive tax is becoming an increasingly important source of income. The tax collected locally is usually a combination of state and local levies, with the local tax producing county and municipal income.

Sales taxes increase with inflation, as do income taxes, and therefore in a sense ride the economy, increasing as costs increase. On the other hand, when consumers are hard-pressed to meet expenditures, they may buy less and this source of income is thereby reduced. The sales tax also fluctuates with the seasons in areas where vacationers and travelers contribute to the economy. It reacts to cost increases. The gasoline tax is a prime example of this; with the increased cost of gasoline, people in hard times buy less gas, thus reducing the tax income from that source. In states that have no income taxes but rely on sales taxes, the fluctuations in revenue have caused serious difficulties as they try to balance their budgets, even forcing some to reduce already allocated appropriations when sales tax collections fall below estimates.

Additional local sources of income include taxes on income from stocks and bonds, on real estate transfers, and fees from the sale of licenses. Fees and licenses, once largely used as a means of regulating service, are now more likely to be expected to cover the cost of the service, or even to provide a modest profit. Fees are also being placed on some services traditionally covered by the municipal or county budget, such as garbage collection and sidewalk maintenance.

There is a strong movement to charge fees for library services as a means of making libraries a pay-as-you-go activity. Charges for non-resident borrowing are fairly common. Fees for specialized services have been imposed for some time and include charges for on-line reference searches, interlibrary loan, and other individualized service. As planners look at local services, library service will receive considerable pressure to "generate additional revenue." As funding becomes increasingly difficult to obtain from traditional sources, librarians will find themselves re-examining traditional position against fees for service. Some have suggested the model in which a basic level of library service is freely available to all but additional services would be fee-based.

The extent to which a library can expect to have its budget requests met is dependent more on the amount of revenue available and the competing priorities than on the worth of the library's program alone. This does not eliminate or reduce the need for careful planning prior to the budget request process, but it does set limits on the support that the administrator can realistically expect to receive.

If the library is chartered to serve a school district, the funds for library support derive from the same tax base as those for the school. In some communities the school district and the city or county government have the same base and taxes are collected on a one-time basis for all services. In other instances the school district serves a population different from the municipal population and school taxes are collected separately. A number of public libraries are organized to serve special districts and are permitted to collect a library levy from those districts. This arrangement is usually made in an area of small communities or a contiguous suburban development where the residents are better served by supporting one library rather than several smaller ones, and a local agreement has been reached on the subject. A number of local services such as fire protection and sewage disposal have been developed and funded in this manner but it is uncommon for libraries.

STATE FUNDING

Public libraries derive a measure of their income from the state, with the average percentage of support to public libraries being just over 13 per cent, although the amount of support varies widely among the states.[3] School media centers are also supported in part from state resources, as are college and university collections.

Although the state has not become as substantial a funding source as many planners have hoped, state support has been influential in developing state-wide cooperative information systems. Recommendations that the state assume responsibility for planning and development have been made for the past fifty years, since Joeckel's studies[4,5] on cooperative services in the 1940s, and states have slowly accepted this responsibility. Some state libraries and library associations initiated studies in the 1940s to determine what their role should be in library planning.

State involvement in public library planning and support did not gain momentum until the enactment of the Library Services Act by the federal government in 1956. LSA funds stimulated state-level efforts to develop and plan for library service. Although some states were already involved in planning for library service, most had it as a low priority item and would not have devoted much effort to it without the stimulus of federal monies. To obtain funding under the federal legislation, states were required to have a state-level agency responsible for library development and to have a long-range plan for library services. These requirements were met by the states with varying degrees of enthusiasm, and planning was carried out with varying levels of expertise. Regional agencies within states took on various shapes and governance structures. In New York, a leader in systems development, twenty-two systems were organized covering the entire state. Governance structures varied. Large metropolitan libraries—the New York Public Library, Brooklyn Public Library and Queens Borough Public Library—were large enough in themselves to qualify as systems. Groupings of libraries devised by county governments became federated systems and groupings that came together because of the cooperative efforts of local libraries became cooperative systems. Each system had its board of trustees selected by the organizing agencies and this body was made responsible for allocating state funds to member libraries according to state guidelines. In other states, system structure is usually more informal, with some major libraries often designated to serve as resource centers for libraries in a particular area.

For a number of states, the long-range planning and the system structure have served as vehicles for allocating state as well as federal dollars. In other states nearly all of the resources allocated are federal dollars, with little or no state input. The decade of the 1980s and the early 1990s have been difficult times for state funding of public libraries as states have had difficulty in meeting their overall needs. New York, Massachusetts, and Michigan have been among the states which have reduced their support of libraries on a state-wide basis, and some other states have held their support at the existing level. The trend in the past decade has been to reduce the level of state support to public libraries. Until the economy becomes stronger than it has been at the beginning of the 1990s, there is little expectation that levels of state support will increase or in many cases remain at the existing level.[6]

As a source of income, state funds are often limited in their use to specific purposes. Examples include the development of long-range plans and facilitating resource-sharing among libraries. In many states, the resources of a local agency cannot be used by people in a jurisdiction whose taxes did not purchase them. In such cases library materials cannot be used outside the purchasing community, but if state funds are involved materials can be used more widely. The state is capable of dealing with situations that involve multi-jurisdictional activities and that require regional solutions. Because state governments tend to be conservative, however, the development of state library policy and state funding programs for libraries has been slow.

Although limited, the state is a source of income for the public library. In terms of actual dollars, the 13 per cent of public library support from state sources has remained relatively stable for the past several years. What must be remembered is that the total dollars available for library service may increase or decrease even though the percentages may not vary. This may make it appear as though state support has increased even though it has actually stayed about the same.

In addition to state monies which may be available to achieve state objectives or federal/state objectives in library service, state legislation in support of other programs may also serve as sources of funds. One such source is funding available in support of the arts. Each state has an Arts Council or similar agency that is responsible for the development and support of programs in its field. A portion of the funding available comes from the National Endowment for the Arts, with the remaining money available from state-appropriated funds. Library programs may qualify for funding to support the arts through lecture series, theater groups or similar activities. Funds are available for artists and for community programs rather than for collection development, although collection development may be a secondary aspect of some proposals.

At the state level, with few exceptions, library and information programs are not well supported. They have few enemies but only a few vocal friends. To many legislators, information service is not a priority item for state support. As is the case with library funding at the local level, when money is in sufficient supply some is available to fund library service, but when funds are limited, library service has a low priority.

FEDERAL FUNDING

Funding from federal sources for public libraries has been available since the mid-1950s. Although federal support of libraries has been minimal, one to two per cent, it has had a major impact on planning and on the development of innovative services. During that time federal aid has had a major impact on public library service, in particular on planning, on regional activities and on building programs. The cause of libraries has had champions in Congress since the 1950s, and a number of programs in support of library service have been proposed and funded. The commitment by successive administrations has varied but in Congress there has been steady support for the concept that the federal government has a role in supporting the information resources of the nation and their accessibility to the citizenry. As we enter the electronic age of networked information, the government is taking a leading role in planning and designing the information infrastructure of the future. Libraries must play a key role in this activity.

The first major categorical funding[7] for libraries was the Library Services Act (P.L. 597), directed toward the support of the public library. Its major purpose was to provide service to those areas not served, in particular to rural areas. Such legislation was first proposed by Joeckel in his 1944 study and further elaborated in his 1948 *National Plan for Public Library Service.* Additional support for federal aid for public library service came from experimental work conducted by the State of New York in the Watertown area. The desirability of federal support of extension service was common to many proposals and recommendations made during the 1940s and 1950s. An added incentive was the publication of a new set of standards for public library service in 1955. At that time, per capita support for libraries was $1.45 nationally, and it was estimated that only about one-quarter of the population received even minimal levels of service.

The Library Services Act provided funds to states and territories to enable them to extend and improve service to areas with populations of 10,000 or less. Congress amended the Act in 1964 to include urban as well as rural districts. The legislation was also extended to include buildings, and became the Library Services and Construction Act (P.L. 91–600).

The long-term benefits of LSCA have been considerable in many states. The federal funds, along with corresponding commitments by some states, have contributed to improving the overall level of local and regional planning. A policy of many state plans was to strengthen existing strong libraries so that they would be able to extend their services.

Title I of LSCA, a matching grant program based on state plans for service, has been an important source of funding for reaching minorities and the disadvantaged. Programs to enlarge, expand or enrich services have been part of statewide plans for service, approved by the state agency. Interlibrary cooperation, such as coordinated information services and consultant services, were also made possible under Title I. Title II, providing matching funds for library construction, was relatively short-lived because of the matching funds requirement, which tended to benefit those communities with at least moderate local resources. Title III funds, for planning, establishing and operating cooperative networks of libraries at local, state, regional or inter-state levels, and including all types of libraries, have become increasingly important as libraries try to cope with mounting costs of materials and services while resources are declining. It also provides a source of funding to support continued networking activities. Title IV is intended to provide funds to supply materials in state-operated or state-supported institutions such as training schools, hospitals and prisons, and to support students in state-sanctioned schools for the handicapped. It also provides funds for service to the physically handicapped and sight-impaired. The emphasis of LSCA is on interlibrary cooperation and on programs for target groups which require special services that are otherwise not adequately funded.

Since 1975 there has been discussion in Congress and within the executive branch as to the future direction of federal support of public library service. The White House Conferences on Libraries and Information Services in 1979 and in 1991 considered alternative ways of funding library service. Although intended to provide overall reviews of the state of library service in the nation, both conferences, because of the large number of representatives from the sectors served by the public and school libraries, focused heavily on the needs of these constituencies. The White House Conferences provided forums for discussion of the federal role in supporting library services and differing views were aired. Despite numerous discussions over the past two decades, including those discussions at the White House Conferences, LSCA continues to be the major federal legislation in support of public libraries.

In addition to the LSCA, major funding for libraries has been available under the Higher Education Act of 1965 (P.L. 89–329) as amended. Intended to support academic institutions and their program efforts, funds have been made available for acquisition of materials and for research and demonstration grants relating to many aspects of information services, particularly resource sharing. This legislation has also provided fellowships for both master's and doctoral study in areas of national shortage such as science information specialists and technical services specialists. This legislation has received continuous funding since its enactment, despite regular challenges.

The National Telecommunications and Information Administration (NTIA) in 1994 announced a competitive grant program whose objectives are to further the goals of the National Information Infrastructure. It provides matching grants to a wide range of agencies including libraries which submit projects that will enhance the delivery of social services and support the formation of an advanced nation-wide telecommunications and information infrastructure. Partnerships joining libraries with other information providing agencies, community groups, or other non-profit groups are encouraged. Funded through the U.S. Department of Commerce, this program provides an opportunity to participate in the information infrastructure of the future.

Legislation supporting elementary and secondary school libraries has been in effect since 1957, first with the National Defense Education Act and later the Elementary and Secondary Education Act. Funds in support of library services were substantial early in the funding period but have declined. During the early years of this legislation, school library resources were increased measurably. This legislation continues to be funded although at a lower level than in the past.

In addition to these sources of library support, there is a wide range of legislation that applies in whole or in part to information services. Although it is possible to some extent to categorize funds available by type of information service, it is preferable to organize sources of funding by function: program development and support, staff support. Resources may be available to libraries as part of a larger grant program such as volunteer workers from the Retired Senior Volunteer Program, the Senior Community Service Employment Program or VISTA, often called the domestic Peace Corps. The Vocational Education Act provides support for technology education demonstrations. The National Institute of Health provides medical library assistance and the Department of Health and Human Services supports programs of excellence in Health Professions Education for Minorities.

The National Endowments for the Arts and Humanities are of

special importance to information-related agencies. The two units, one supporting the arts and the other supporting the humanities, make funds available to support artists, the development of humanities resources and the presentation of creative works to the community. The focus is not on the library but on the artist and the artist's product, but the support structure used to develop and make that product available has often been a library.

When seeking funds in support of specific program objectives, more and more institutions are partnering with others with like objectives, thus indicating a level of interest, support and cooperation beyond a single institution. A community information service proposal would be strengthened by a partnership among selected community program providers and the library. For example, a health and wellness awareness proposal would be much stronger if supported by health agencies in the community and community action groups as well as by the library.

A second type of legislation in support of information services is directed toward making available publications, statistical services, educational programs, exhibits and other types of materials. Nearly every government agency provides information reporting its activities and services. Much of this is free and, if selected carefully, it can enrich the library's reference resources. The Library of Congress, the U.S. Government Printing Office and other federal information agencies provide services which may be of value to the individual library.

From 1972 to 1986, revenue sharing, a non-categorical aid plan using a formula based on population, tax collections and categorical income, was a welcome source of state and local income. During the early years of revenue sharing, approximately five billion dollars per year were allocated. Libraries benefited from revenue sharing particularly in acquiring new buildings and renovating existing buildings. Never universally popular in federal government circles, revenue sharing was terminated as federal resources became increasingly scarce.

FUNDING FROM PRIVATE SOURCES

Private foundations have for the past century or more served as a source of funds for services directed toward the improvement of the quality of life. Library and information service meets this criterion. There are more than 26,000 foundations with a combined wealth of more than 40 billion dollars. The bulk of that wealth is in a limited number of agencies, including the Carnegie, Rockefeller, and Ford Foundations. Approximately two-thirds of the foundations are small and have assets of less than $250,000. The large portion of foundation resources is tied up in assets such as mortgages, stocks, bonds and other income-producing ventures, with corporate stock the largest single investment.

Each foundation has specific types of programs and projects which it favors for funding. Application is made to the trustees or the directors of the foundation, and they determine the applicability of the request to the foundation's funding objectives. As foundation assets are largely intangible and are dependent upon the market and the state of the economy, the amount of money available from a particular foundation in any one year will vary. Funds were readily available from a number of foundations in the 1960s, but as the economy tightened in the 1970s and 1980s profits on investments declined, and funds available to support the foundations' objectives were reduced. The difficulties experienced by many corporations as they respond to the need to downsize, to reorganize and reinvent themselves for the twenty-first century have limited their ability to pay dividends to stockholders. Traditionally well-endowed foundations may become less affluent; meanwhile, new foundations are being established by the newly affluent information industry giants.

Foundations support a wide range of activities and provide an opportunity to carry out research and support activities in addition to those for which public dollars are available. Many foundations support activities within a region; others are concerned with innovation in knowledge areas such as the sciences and social sciences. A strong element in the giving patterns of many foundations is the improvement of social conditions. Many foundations, for example, focus on health-related concerns and on education. Several foundations, including Ford and Carnegie, have long-term commitments which are given priority over annual grant requests. Education, which receives nearly one-third of foundation funds, is the area most vulnerable to grant reductions because of the amount of money involved and the degree to which various educational groups have come to rely on foundations, both for continuing support and for new grant-supported activities.

Because foundation resources are tied to the economy and because of federal requirements for reporting by foundations, it is possible to predict, to a degree, the probability of success when requesting funds.

In addition to being aware of the level of money available from a foundation, individuals seeking support should study the purpose of the foundation and its pattern of giving. Before approaching a foundation, the grant seekers should know what activities the foundation supports and the extent to which those activities and the priorities they represent are in line with the priorities of their own agencies.

The library manager or policy maker concerned with obtaining foundation funds for special projects can obtain up-to-date and relatively complete information through the Foundation Center, which maintains national collections in New York and Washington and regional collections throughout the country. These centers provide, through publications and other channels, descriptive information on foundations, their resources and giving patterns, and requirements for making application. The Foundation's data bank is available on-line and can be searched from any location on the basis of key word, foundation name, or recipient name. The data base includes descriptions of grants by large foundations and annual reporting of foundations based on their Internal Revenue Service returns.

A number of national foundations have a pattern of giving that includes libraries and information support services, and a number of local and regional foundations have given to libraries as a means of enriching their communities. The Carnegie Foundation, since its establishment in 1911, has included libraries and higher education among its priorities. The funds available in recent decades have been for research that would benefit the profession as a whole, such as the sponsoring of the Public Library Inquiry in the late 1940s. The W. K. Kellogg Foundation is concerned with the role of information in our increasingly information-rich society and is particularly concerned with issues dealing with access to information by the public. National level foundations are most likely to support activities which improve information services rather than the activities of a particular institution. Regional foundations are more likely to support individual libraries in their area.

Businesses and industrial corporations have often set up foundations as a means of supporting communities within which they are located. These serve both to enrich the community and to enhance the image of the company. Company foundations usually have no endowment and the funds vary from year to year depending on the annual profit margin of the company. Continuing good relationships with the local business community is an important part of the local political and financial responsibilities of library managers and fund raisers, who need to be in a position to learn about local sources of private support and to have favorable access when making grant requests.

The way in which library managers go about seeking external funds varies, but many large libraries have a development officer responsible for identifying sources of funding and for seeking out funds to meet library needs. In academic institutions, this individual works closely with the college or university development officer; in the public library, this individual works closely with the library director and the board of trustees. Depending upon the structure within which the library is located, the types of potential donors will vary. Grants from foundations are possible for most libraries provided that the funds they are seeking are in support of a program or activity on the foundation's priority list. Grants from regional or local foundations or local industry are available to improve the quality of life in a particular area. Alumni donations, both from alumni organizations and individual donors, are an important source, and over the past several years academic libraries have sometimes fared well in their efforts to obtain funding from private sources. Academic and public library collection development, particularly in the area of special collections, is an area which frequently gains support from private donors. Large research libraries have been successful in this regard. Although at one time building programs were well supported by private donors, this is no longer a priority.

Foundations were established, among other reasons, to provide support for research and to further social objectives outside the structure provided for by public monies. Foundation funds were seen as an alternative to public funding, and although they are not in opposition to one another, there has traditionally been little cooperation between the two. This has begun to change recently as planners have recommended funding packages for programs that include elements of both private and public funding. Start-up funds for a project may be requested under a federal grant and, as the project progresses, part of it may qualify for funding under a private foundation. When the emphasis is on planning, the funding sources can be mixed, in response to program objectives and available funding. The complexity of the accounting may be increased but this is not a major problem.

The balance between seeking external support and maintaining current levels of basic support is difficult to maintain. If a library is successful in obtaining external "soft" money to support aspects of its program, its basic support budget may be cut. If a library does not seek out added funds, its program will suffer, and in addition the library manager may well be chided for lack of effort. It must be made clear to the primary funding agency that external support provides supplemental money for purposes specified in the grant. External funding is typically not for general operating purposes, and should not be seen as a way of reducing levels of general operating support.

CHARGES FOR SERVICE

A further means of obtaining funds to cover the expense of providing information service is to charge the user. Tax-supported information services are subsidized by an overall charge to taxpayers in the area served by the library. Many academic institutions include in their fees a surcharge that is intended to subsidize use of the academic library. Other information services are in one way or another supported by organizational fees or dues paid by members. Those not subject to this general subsidy may be required to pay a user fee.

In the case of public libraries, the move of many residents from urban to suburban locations has removed them from the tax rolls, but many may still use urban services, including library service.

Most public libraries charge non-resident fees for service. Many academic libraries charge use fees, as do specialized organizations. These charges may be flat fees for a specified period of time or may be pro-rated according to anticipated level of use. Traditionally non-resident fee setting has been used as a control mechanism limiting use rather than a true reflection of the cost of using resources. Although raising the level of non-resident fees to cover the cost of service would make them prohibitively expensive, a fee structure that is based on levels and types of use could be considered. In addition to reviewing the purpose and application of the fee structure, the funding agency should be made aware of the levels of non-resident use and how the charges for non-resident use are applied. Fee adjustments, indeed the existence of fees, can cause negative reaction. The library manager needs the support of the parent organization when setting and imposing such charges. Public awareness, as well as awareness by the funding agency, of the cost of information services and the extent to which imposed fees cover those costs is important.

Fees are often imposed for specialized services such as on-line searches, interlibrary loan, or reserving popular material. Arguments for and against the concept of charging for information services have been present in the literature for some time. As library budgets shrink and as the demand for searching of on-line data bases increases, there has been a gradual movement toward charging for this specialized service as it is seen as a means of providing additional services and products without diluting basic library services. The price charged may or may not reflect the actual cost of the on-line search. Unlike the private sector, where fees are related to cost, publicly supported libraries are less likely to charge the full cost. When fees reflect the cost of a search, for example, they often cover only time on the system, printout and/or mailing costs. Cost of the information professional's time, cost of thesauri needed to develop the search, and other related costs may not be charged to the user. Those libraries which have charged full cost have not necessarily experienced a drop in requests for searches, as library patrons seem to expect higher costs for electronically accessible information. A number of libraries have instituted services for business clients and provide a range of services for which the clients pay a flat annual fee or on the basis of fees for services provided.

Fee-based information services, both those within a library and those provided by an information broker, have doubled in number in the past five years and continue to grow. These services provide on-line and manual searching, photocopying of documents and document delivery. Many libraries have extensive video collections and rental fees are a steady source of income.

Some planners have made much of the benefits that will accrue if the library charges for specialized services. They assert that charging for service can promote efficiency in library operations, that high-cost services will be paid for by the individuals benefiting from the service rather than the cost being distributed among all users, and finally, that user charges are a source of revenue that will rescue the library from the effects of reduced budgets. Although there is some merit to these arguments, it is difficult to carry them through to the conclusion that information service will be rescued from final doom by the simple application of user fees. As one part of the overall package of information service options and one source of income to support the information service program, fees are a consideration.

The funding for an information service comes primarily from the parent funding agency, be it local government, academic budget, association resources or other source. Federal and state grants, as well as grants from foundations, are special-purpose allocations over and above the basic support package. Gifts, bequests and other grants can be important sources of funds but they too are apt to be for special purposes. Fees for service are directed toward special services and are therefore not an integral part of general operating revenue. The health of the organization is determined by the primary funding agent. Other resources enrich a program but do not maintain its viability.

NOTES

1) National Center for Educational Statistics, *Public Libraries in the United States: 1991.* Washington, D.C.: U.S. Department of Education, Office of Research and Improvement, 1993, p. 36.

2) Ira Sharansky, *The Politics of Taxing and Spending.* Indianapolis: Bobbs-Merrill, 1969, p. i.

3) National Center for Educational Statistics, *Public Libraries in the United States: 1991,* p. 36.

4) Carleton B. Joeckel, ed. *Library Extension, Problems and Solution: Papers Presented Before the Library Institute at the University of Chicago, August 21–26.* Chicago: American Library Association, 1946.

5) Carleton B. Joeckel, ed. *A National Plan for Public Library Service.* Chicago: American Library Association, 1948.

6) Christinger Tomer, "The Effects of the Recession on Academic and Public Libraries," in *The Bowker Annual; 37th Edition.* New Providence, N.J.: Bowker, 1992, pp. 77–78.

7) Categorical funding is funding where resources are to be used for purposes specified by the legislation. Non-categorical funding can be used at the discretion of the recipient.

VIII

FINANCIAL CONTROL

Reporting expenditures and accounting for the funds entrusted to the library serve a number of purposes: financial, evaluative, and political. Accounting and expenditure reporting complete the planning cycle, in that results are used to evaluate, refine, and modify the plan as reflected in the budget. The administrator is thus ready for the next planning cycle. For many years emphasis was on expenditure, and planning aspects received less attention. Both require close attention if the agency is to be at once accountable and forward-looking.

DEVELOPMENT OF THE REPORTING SYSTEM

The financial information system that exists or should exist is designed to meet a variety of needs. Those budgeting systems—PBS, PPBS—devised and implemented in the past decades have had as one of their major objectives the improvement of management of resources. Long-range planning for services, estimation of cost programs, and development of line-item budgets for each program were required. Evaluation in relation to objectives was built into each system. All of this is necessary and helpful in modern budgeting and planning.

Once a budget resulting from the long-range plan of an agency is approved, the funding authority sets an appropriation level. The appropriation is formally adopted and serves as the upper limit at which that service will be supported. The financial management system is set up in such a way as to insure that funds are spent on the goods and services for which they are allocated, and that those responsible for spending public monies are doing so with the best interests of the taxpayer in mind. Not only should the financial management system maintain control of expenditures; the information derived from the system should be in a form that facilitates evaluation. The evaluative data are then used to modify the long-range plan through the development of unit-cost and cost-benefit factors.

A final requirement of the financial management system is that data for reporting to external groups are available. The format and complexity of the reporting may vary with the intended audience, the citizenry or the funding authority, but in either case the reporting should be accurate, clearly written, and easy to understand by the target audience.

Good accounting practices and appropriate reporting systems have similar components regardless of the environment within which an agency operates, and they are regulated by standards imposed by groups responsible for uniform accounting practices. There are, however, different emphases in application in profit and non-profit organizations. The emphasis here is on the non-profit organization, which has been defined as ". . . an economic entity that provides, *without profit to the owners,* a service beneficial to society and that is financed by equity interests that cannot be sold or traded by individuals or profit seeking entities."[1]

Non-profit organizations may be voluntarily supported, as are private colleges, hospitals and churches, as well as private associations. These may or may not be self-sustaining. Those categorized as involuntarily supported are the government entities including public colleges, public schools, public libraries and other public information services. These are not self-supporting and require regular funding. Libraries, depending upon the governance structure of the parent institution, can fall within either category. The non-profit agency may be controlled by a voting membership or by representatives of the taxpayer. Decisions made are intended to respond to the general needs of the community rather than to a profit motive, as would be the case with a for-profit information service.

When setting up an accounting and reporting system for a non-profit organization, it is important to identify the purposes and the intended outcomes of the system. Few planners are in a position to design a new system but many find themselves in the position of having to evaluate the current situation and adapt existing procedures as best they can to emerging needs.

FUND ACCOUNTING

Income may derive from a number of sources. For many libraries, the major source of income is tax revenues. The parent organization categorizes these revenues by their source: sales taxes, property tax, or income tax. The library reporting system may require only that an item listing contributions from local government be included. For the public library this is typically the largest single source of income. Other sources include involuntary income such as fines and fees, and voluntary income such as grants and gifts. Income from state sources or federal sources is listed separately. Finally, a library may have investments which earn income.

Each source of income must be listed. If there are funds that carry limitations on their use, this is noted. Otherwise it is assumed that all income goes toward the general operating fund. Special purpose funds that cannot be used for general operating expenses are treated separately and income and expenditures are recorded for each fund in accordance with the terms of the fund.

A fund has been defined by the National Committee on Governmental Accounting as

> an independent fiscal and accounting entity with a self-balancing set of accounts recording cash and/or other resources together with all related liabilities, obligations, reserves and equities which are segregated for the purpose of carrying on specific activities or attaining certain objectives in accordance with special regulations, restrictions or limitations.[2]

A fund can be the result of a bequest to the library, a special purpose grant, a gift or other income. Common to all are specific requirements concerning expenditures. Some are sums of money to be used for specific purposes, others are to be invested, with only the interest available for use. The manager is legally and morally committed to spend according to the specifications of the fund, be it in support of collection development, an educational program, or some other specified activity.

Each fund has separate accounting and reporting. Its identity is maintained at all times. Federal or state grants to carry out specific programs are treated in the same manner as funds, and separate records are maintained for each in accordance with regulations covering the use of allocations. An income statement thus consists of two general sections: one listing income that contributes to the general operation of the library and a second section listing all special-purpose funds and income derived from them during the time period covered by the income statement.

If the library has a capital fund, it is typically dedicated to a specific objective such as a new building. Income received is credited to that fund and held separate from operating income in the same way as other funds.

REPORTING STANDARDS

There is no one set of generally accepted reporting standards for non-business organizations. However, accounting principles have been published for several types of non-profit agencies and they tend to be fairly consistent. Although several states have statutes governing financial accounting principles for government units, there is limited consistency among them. Several states have either no practices prescribed by law or prescribed practices that are inconsistent with the principles approved by the AICPA (American Institute of Certified Public Accountants) or the National Council of Governmental Accounting. A number of audit guides have been published by federal agencies. As a result, the financial systems of many non-profit organizations have not been established according to approved standards. Many organizations are not audited regularly by certified public accountants and some that are may have difficulty in working with accountants who are more familiar with business accounting practices. A major difference is that non-profit agencies require both internal and external reporting, while for-profit agencies are relatively unconcerned with external reporting.

USERS OF THE REPORTING SYSTEM

"The users of accounting data are always interested in knowing the extent to which the objectives of an economic entity have been achieved and the amount of resources available to the entity for that purpose."[3] As far as possible, accounting and reporting practices should be developed and designed both to make available information on the financial condition of the organization and to serve as a means of monitoring it. The information and the format of its presentation can best be determined by identifying those who will be using it. These user groups include both internal management (director and department heads) and external management (city government, boards of trustees, university administration, etc.). The public which supports the service through taxes or fees also has the right to know the results of its support. Each constituency uses the information for different purposes and each benefits from a different type or format for reporting. Differences may be in the amount of information provided or in the manner of its presentation.

External management groups are usually the policy-making authorities. They need to know about the overall health of the organization in general terms. What has been accomplished with the funds provided? This question may be broken down into additional questions: what would be the effects of reduced funding on delivery of services, or what results might be achieved with the addition of funds? The policy makers expect information in measurable terms indicating the way in which funds have been used to carry out policies and the results achieved in terms of service. ". . . Reports of any resource conversion enterprise should be organized to show, insofar as is practically possible, the relationship between achievements (represented by revenues realized or the value of services rendered) and efforts (measured in terms of the costs of realizing revenues and rendering services).[4] Reporting information is provided for both income and its sources and expenditures and their results. The amount of information is limited to what is necessary in order to review policy decisions and plan for future activities.

Internal managers require the same policy information. In addition, they require detailed data on day-to-day operations. Each department head needs full information on the way in which resources within the department are used and the results that accrue. This information from each program and department, cumulated in a slightly generalized form, provides the director and administrative staff with appropriate information to plan and monitor services. The reporting activity and the evaluative process which leads from the reporting are integral parts of the program and performance budgeting systems.

Those who support the service through taxation, fees or other means have the right to know how their money is spent and the results of the expenditure. If a library wishes to continue to be funded, it must continually prove that it is worthy of support. Reports to the constituent support group must be organized to respond to the need for justification. Information service is a public good that benefits society and the individual. As such, in the abstract most people say that it is deserving of support. In times of financial stress, however, such a blanket expectation of approval is unrealistic. Supporters expect more specific answers to such questions as: do we have enough, too much, or too little information service available? Is the service provided in the best and most efficient manner? Is the library using its resources in the way intended by the taxpayer? Policy is made to give the managers of the organization guidelines by which to provide service that meets the needs of the constituents. They are the ultimate policy makers and express their satisfaction or dissatisfaction by the level of financial support they are willing to provide.

Data provided to this group should respond to policy questions in terms as quantifiable as possible. Services are difficult to measure in many instances, but it is possible to calculate the number of people served, the range of their information needs, the size of the information collection and the expertise necessary to respond to those needs. The percentage of resources devoted to any one aspect of library services can be indicated. Although there may be variations in what is included in the calculations, the overall questions of how was money spent and who was served can be answered.

The efficiency with which services are performed is also of concern to the constituency. Information service is labor-intensive, with two-thirds or more of the operating budget going for personnel costs. This needs to be justified, as does the overhead cost of administration. A reference specialist may be easier to justify than a second associate director.

Activity-based accounting, which reviews activities and determines their value to the customer, provides a Total Quality Management approach to accounting as a means of informing both the organization and its clientele as to the worth of their services. In this mode, each function of each staff member is analyzed to determine if it is needed by the customer. By looking at activities in relation to their value to the customer, one is then able to improve those activities of greatest perceived value and eliminate or downsize those of lesser perceived value.[5]

In answering the questions of constituents, administrators are finding answers for themselves as well. Both groups expect to have a lean and well-run organization. Although the constituents need the same sort of information that their representatives in the external management or policy-making group need, they are interested in brief reports and direct responses to their questions rather than any extended reporting. The general public, those not necessarily supporting the service but with an interest in and concern for information services and its delivery, has similar but more general concerns. In the public library, the constituent group and the general public are the same. In other settings, such as the college or the school library, the constituent user group is smaller than the group interested in the service.

Additional groups that may be interested in financial reports are those which provide goods and services to the library: jobbers, utility companies and other contractors. They are concerned with the economic stability of the organization and the extent of their risk in extending services. The library can be seen as an efficient operating unit where policies are sound, objectives are met and reporting is prompt and accurate; missing these factors, it can be seen as an inefficiently run organizational unit. If there is need to borrow money for expansion or technological development, the reputation of the organization and the availability of careful reporting are important factors in determining the chances of obtaining it.

REPORTING FORMATS

The National Committee on Governmental Accounting has proposed a standardized format for financial reporting.[6] It consists of an introductory section, a financial section, and a statistical section. Applied to libraries, the introductory section would include a brief description of the library's structure and would identify any agencies related to the library such as a quasi-independent archive, a specialized information center, or another agency within the same governance structure. A description of the way in which agencies within the governance structure report their financial activity should be included to the extent necessary for clarity. The dates of the fiscal years, any specialized accounting practices and any changes in accounting practices from prior reports would be indicated. The report should provide a clear but brief description of the manner in which the budget is prepared, administered and reported. A similar description is necessary for the capital budget, and any possible links between the operating budget and the capital budget should be mentioned. Finally, the report should include a summary comparison of annual operating budgets over several years so that trends of expenditures are readily observable.

The statistical section is a statement of trends and of the degree to which income and expenditures meet state or national standards. It would include a review of income from local, state, and federal sources and changes in levels of support. It would also include an analysis of the effects of inflation on actual expenditures, the progress of the library in meeting ALA or other standards, and other analyses helpful for planning and directing library services.

In order to insure consistency in reporting, all reports should conform to the same guidelines. As more and more libraries and their governing entities move toward automated systems for maintaining records, single-source reports are becoming the norm. The same information is presented for each agency, differing only in the degree of specificity and in the way in which it is presented. The data used in preparing reports must be both consistent and objective; otherwise it is not possible to compare data from various sections of the report or from several reporting agencies. Reported information must also be consistent over time so that the data for one year can be compared to those for another.

State or municipal regulations may include formats for financial reporting and most certainly include a requirement for annual reporting. The distribution of the reports is also usually determined by legal requirements. Distribution is usually required for certain individuals and groups and is optional for others.

The format for reporting must be consistent with approved accounting procedures. This requirement is typically part of the regulations for reporting that are provided by the parent governing body. The standard format includes a *balance sheet* showing resources and obligations of the organization; an *operating statement* giving all revenue and expenditure data; a statement of the sources and uses for any *special purpose funds;* and a statement of changes in *fund balances* for these special purpose funds. Financial statements should show total operational accountability. Because there are various sources of funding for many libraries, reporting should show both the uses of general purpose monies supplied by the parent organization and those of special grants and funds.

ACCOUNTING

Accounting is the technical aspect of reporting, a standardized means of recording quantitative data about the income and expenditure of resources of an organization, a way of recording its assets and liabilities consistently over a period of time. It is the basis for developing reports to be distributed to various interest groups. Financial accounting has been called score-keeping, keeping track of where dollars come from and where they go. Managers use the reports as a way of monitoring income and expenditures and expect the reports to be an accurate reflection of the financial health of the organization.

Cost Accounting—Cost accounting is defined as the art of determining the cost of a product, a service or an activity. It is used for budgeting, cost analysis, comparison with standards, and general comparisons of actual and historical costs.

Historical cost—is the cost of an item or service at the time of its purchase for use, and is currently accepted as the base for recording and accounting of assets and expenditures.

Standard costs—are a determination of what costs for an identifiable output or activity should be, and can be either the result of detailed study or informed estimate. They serve as a measure against which historical costs can be reviewed.

Unit costs—are the costs of providing a specified unit of service or product, and are the most common means of expressing costs. They are used for general planning, for annual budget development, for comparison with organizations providing similar services, and as a means of keeping expenditures in line with the budget.

Reviews of the accounting activities of educational and research institutions, including libraries, have shown that the levels of sophistication of the library component are relatively low, with projected disbursements simply matched to projected receipts. In this situation little real effort is made to use accounting to price services and to determine their actual cost. In recent years, more and more of the information services have been reviewed to determine actual cost, particularly in areas where fees are most likely to be charged, such as on-line searching and interlibrary loan. While at one time librarians were seen as very reluctant to determine the actual cost of services, this is no longer the case. Management of information services is becoming much more sophisticated.

There is still a concern in some areas that costing out information services will show that these services are not cheap and that were the funding agency to know the real costs, it might be reluctant to support them. But as there is no way of placing an accurate dollar value on a "public good," there is no accurate way to value a service which in dollar cost alone appears too high. In addition to the simple unit cost of a service, the benefits to the public of delivering this service must be added.

As has been stated, major purposes of reporting are evaluation and comparison with similar organizations or similar activities. As part of the movement toward Total Quality Management, benchmarking "an ongoing, systematic process for measuring and comparing the work processes of one organization to those of another by bringing an external focus to the internal activities, functions or operations" sets an external standard for evaluation.[7]

Benchmarks set a standard of performance against which one can compare like practices within an organization, compare performance between like organizations or identify the best performer. It answers the questions: how well are we doing in relation to others? who is doing it best? and what are they doing that we can apply to our situation so that we can do it better? This search for best practice leads to improvement in the organization's performance.

Use of accounting data to identify actual costs, to evaluate services and to compare success in delivering services provides essential information for overall planning and decision-making. An understanding of how resources were used and what was achieved allows the library manager to make the strongest possible case for budget requests.

Accrual Accounting and Cash Accounting—The accrual concept has been generally accepted, as it provides a means for reporting liabilities, such as accounts payable, and assets in addition to cash, thus providing a truer statement of worth than cash accounting. Important to the concept of accrual accounting is the use of terms *expense* (a measure of the materials and services used during a particular period) and *expenditure* (the incurring of a liability not necessarily limited to a particular period). Accrual accounting takes both of these into consideration. Expenses include the cost of salaries, communications, and other costs incurred in a specific time period. Expenditures include materials to be used over a considerable period, long-term insurance policies, service contracts, and other costs that are committed for some time. The cost of supplies for inventory can also be included under expenditures as their use may be over a long term. Annual reports record both the expenses incurred in a year and expenditure incurred for a longer period.

Agencies funded on an annual basis may not be able to save funds for long-term expenditures such as equipment. Fiscal policy in most government units is that expenditures must equal income, and tax rates are set to meet this objective. This enforcement of the requirement that tax-supported organizations live within their annual income prevents saving resources for items that will be used over the long-term but are too expensive to purchase in one year. Annual funding can be and often is a deterrent to long-range planning.

The general trend in the non-profit sector is toward a full accounting of all resources rather than a cash basis record, and an adherence to the standards of the Federal Accounting Standards Board. The purpose is to provide financial statements which will answer the questions the various users of reporting data are asking or should be asking. "The ultimate objective of financial reporting should be to provide information useful for evaluating management effectiveness in utilizing resources under its control to satisfy users' needs, whether economic or social."[8]

This is much easier to state as an objective than to implement, as the objectives of library service are difficulty to quantify in terms of value. Again, this is a difficulty inherent in evaluating a public good. The reporting process, however, does provide standards for comparison of services. The reports of a number of libraries can be used to develop statistical profiles of a region. Comparative data on funding status, salary levels and materials expenditures can be determined by reviewing a number of reports from similar organizations. Data on larger public libraries in the South have been collected and published by the Memphis and Shelby Co. (TN) Public Library for a number of years, and similar data have been collected by Fort Wayne, Indiana's public library staff. These provide planning data for particular regions. This general information is useful in preparing planning and budgeting documents. It is helpful to know how institutions of a similar size are spending the resources available to them for library service. The funding they receive can also provide helpful comparisons for institutions of similar size. Because of the possible inconsistency in reporting, these data may not be as accurate as one would wish for benchmarking purposes but they will give some fairly good comparative data.

Depreciation Accounting—In reporting activities, certain techniques are employed to adjust figures recording assets and liabilities so as to allow for as accurate a statement of actual worth as possible. Among these techniques are depreciation accounting, which takes into account the wearing out of buildings, equipment, and materials, and reports their worth in relation to decreasing value; and inflation accounting, which takes into consideration the reduced value of dollars because of inflation.

Depreciation accounting in the not-for-profit sector is not formally approved by most experts. It is generally agreed that depreciation of fixed assets should be recorded, but only informally and not as part of the regular reporting system. Those who oppose formal accounting of depreciation in not-for-profit agencies contend that it serves no useful purpose. Not-for-profit organizations are service organizations and therefore have no profits. Since depreciation is a means of charging the use of fixed assets against revenues, and since libraries do not produce revenues beyond possible charges for service, the activity is pointless. Not-for-profit agencies are recorded as operating on a year-to-year basis at the level of funding provided by taxpayers or other supporters. Depreciation is a multi-year activity and is difficult to mesh with the year-to-year funding reality. A further argument against depreciation accounting is that it assumes replacement of an asset once it has reached the end of its useful life. No such assurance exists in tax-supported agencies. A bond issue may be passed for a new building and funds for new equipment may be available when needed, but one cannot depend on it. A further argument against depreciation is that assets held by an agency may not all be essential to its operation; they may be the result of political decisions, either wise or unwise, and assessing depreciation costs for all of them is unnecessary. Others argue that depreciation is difficult to calculate and that no positive result is achieved that cannot be achieved by informal reporting outside the regular budgeting and reporting system.

Those who favor a formal reporting of depreciation contend that whether the purpose of the organization is service or profit, there is a need for a determination of the availability and use of resources. Including the use of assets when determining unit costs provides a more accurate measure of actual program costs, and an awareness of the value and life of assets is essential to efficient planning. Stewardship of resources is part of the charge to managers of not-for-profit organizations. Either in the formal reporting system, or separately, the status of all assets should be reported regularly. Cash flow reporting and its variations are incomplete and do not reflect the total worth of an organization or the total cost of services. Although complete accuracy in reporting depreciation may indeed not be possible, a general indication of the rate at which assets are used is useful both in calculating unit costs and in planning for replacement. The recommendations of the American Accounting Association are that:

> 1) The accounting records and related reports of a not-for-profit organization should disclose the cost of or use or consumption of the assets allocated to services and/or time periods as appropriate by an acceptable depreciation technique;

> 2) Depreciation accounting should be recognized as an integral part of accounting for resources. (Because statutory and regulatory requirements for property accounting cannot be ignored, not-for-profit organizations may find it necessary to make multiple recordings and disclosures of individual transactions.) Where there are specific legal prohibitions against formally recording and reporting depreciation, not-for-profit organizations should use supplementary records and statements to the extent necessary to furnish interested parties with relevant fixed asset depreciation data.[9]

Inflation Accounting—Inflation accounting is a response to the difficulty of using standard accounting and reporting systems in a period of rising process. Inflation has been a factor in the planning, budgeting, funding cycle for some time, and can be expected to continue to be so. Accounting and reporting are based on the principle of historic cost, the principle that the value of assets is determined by their value at the time of purchase. Liabilities are shown at their monetary value. This type of accounting ignores inflation and the effects of price changes on the purchasing power or on the value of assets.

There are a number of ways to deal with the changes in prices due to inflation and to report the effects. The first is to adjust historical dollar amounts to reflect changes in general price levels. The changes can be stated in terms of units of money or in terms of general purchasing power spent for the object of the measurement, such as books and magazines. Adjustment of historical dollar amounts is based on the assumption that there is relative stability in the size of the measuring unit, but this is not necessarily the case since the purchasing power of the dollar is not stable. One way to deal with this is to report historical cost in terms of units of general purchasing power rather than in dollar units. The dollars of equivalent purchasing power would then reflect a uniform measuring unit. Those advocating this type of reporting would use the GNP Implicit Price Deflator Index from the Department of Commerce or some other useful index. "Because accounting information is intended to be used in making current decisions, it seems reasonable that accounting reports should be stated in terms of current dollars, the terms in which the decision maker is most likely to be thinking."[10]

A second way of dealing with the effects of inflation is through current pricing of specific items. This method is less satisfactory than a general change from historical to current costs; not all items change in price at the same rate and pricing of specific items can skew results. Book and periodical prices have increased more rapidly than the rate of inflation, while there has been a decrease in the cost of some computer hardware. Reporting on such items individually does not provide the overall view necessary to planning.

A third type of inflation accounting involves recording the current prices of specific items and adjusting for changes in the general price level. This method is based on the premise that money has value in relation to what it can buy and that historical amounts need to be adjusted in order to reflect current purchasing power. The general purchasing power of the dollar is ever-changing and if one does not take this into consideration, records can be distorted. The choice of price index can be a problem because each has a bias in its composition.

Further, inflation affects services differently, depending upon the amount of change in the service, the resources needed to perform the service, and the condition of supplies and equipment involved.

In order to restate historical dollars in dollars of uniform purchasing power for the current reporting period, adjustments are made in accordance with an index that reflects changes in the purchasing power of the dollar. The historical amount and the date it was fixed must be known. The historical amount is then multiplied by a fraction, the numerator of which is the index for the most recent balance sheet date and the denominator of which is the index for the date of the historical amount.[11] The cost of an asset acquired for $10,000 during year 5 could be adjusted to reflect year 15 dollars in the following manner:

$$\frac{\text{Index at end of year 15} \times \$10000}{\text{Index at date of acquisition (year 5)}} = \begin{array}{l} \text{cost of asset in end of} \\ \text{year 15 dollars} \end{array}$$

The index most often consulted is the GNP Implicit Price Deflator. If that is not available for the period reviewed, the most recent index is used. The reporting sheet resulting from this will state both historical cost and adjusted costs to reflect current value.

Responses to the use of inflation accounting vary both in terms of the entire system and more specifically in terms of the appropriate index to use and the bias that this choice may inject into the record. The adjustments made to the reporting data by calculating against a standard general index result in a set of reports reflecting change in the general purchasing power of the dollar. They are a variation of the adjustments possible if one sets a base year and then reports subsequent years' financial statements in relation to that. For example, 1990 could be set as a base year and reporting throughout the decade would be in relation to 1990 dollars.

There is general agreement that inflation has distorted the financial reporting of not-for-profit organizations and that some form of supplemental reporting is required in order to include the effects of inflation on both income and expenditure in planning. Calculating current value information for some or all parts of the reports available to managers, planners and policy makers is one way of providing such information. These calculations may vary with the items selected and with the index applied, but they should be useful in providing qualified planning data.

LIMITATIONS OF EXISTING REPORTING SYSTEMS

The current state of many library reporting systems is a deterrent to good planning. Categories for income and expenditures for library services are often prescribed by regulations of a local government, an academic institution, or other agency. They may have been in place for decades, and may include, for example, a line for recording gifts but no space to record money received through grants and contracts. In the expenditure line, often the only information materials item listed is books. Where is one to record expenditures for tapes, videodiscs, database services and other non-book information. Inappropriate categories for reporting may also result from management studies of an overall organization conducted by experts whose knowledge of information service is limited.

When they are locked into appropriate pigeonholes it is nearly impossible to record the financial transactions of a library with any degree of accuracy. The problem is similar to that encountered in preparing a budget geared to archaic or non-relevant categories. The only viable solution is to format reports twice, once to reflect actual income and expenditures, and once to conform to the demands of the parent organization. In a small information service this may be merely a nuisance, but for larger enterprises the burden of dual reporting may be unbearable. The problem is not universal but it affects many libraries, the degree of the problem depending upon the rigidity of the parent organization's reporting system.

The system that is used for reporting must reflect, as faithfully as possible, through quantitative measures, the economic facts it represents. Some values that cannot be expressed in quantitative terms are still essential to the reporting system. These include community attitude toward the service, the productivity of internal working relationships, the quality of service provided and similar variables. Often it is these latter elements that provide the real picture of the status of the organization.

ACCOUNTABILITY

Library services, whether linked to profit enterprises or public sector organizations, are subject to demands for accountability. In the case of for-profit enterprises, there is a need to indicate that the funds spent for information services resulted in economic benefits to the company. In the case of not-for-profit organizations there is a need to account for the use of public or donated funds as well as a need to demonstrate that the outcome of providing funding is a better-educated student, greater university research productivity, or a more informed citizenry. Where initially greater emphasis was placed on fiscal accountability monitored through periodic reporting of account balances and other required reports, there has lately been increased emphasis on the more difficult task of showing how the library has made a difference in the institution in which it resides and in the lives of those using the library. The emphasis on outcomes of library involvement in academic efforts is increasing as parents want to see value for the dollars they spend on tuition, and as accrediting bodies look at outcomes of the educational process rather than looking at the size of the library and assuming that it is adequate to the educational tasks. The demand for accountability—how it has changed the lives of the residents of its community—is beginning to be experienced by the public library as well.

Boards of trustees, library directors and other managers are accountable to the legislative body and funding agency for compliance with laws, regulations and policies. Where such compliance is quantifiable, it becomes part of the accounting and reporting system. Managers are also accountable for the ways in which they use the resources entrusted to them. The greater the efficiency in the use of always scarce resources to achieve objectives, the greater the potential benefit. Efficiency can be measured through output (increased output with stable input), through input (specify levels of performance and vary input until the least amount of resources is required to achieve output), through a mixture of the two, and through the concept of optimal efficiency. Optimal efficiency is the level of efficiency where both quality and quantity of benefits are at the highest possible level given the limitations of resources available. This latter measure is program-oriented rather than task- or process-oriented and therefore is most useful to policy makers. The purpose of each of these measures is to insure the efficient use of funds in providing economical service. Implicit in this emphasis on economy is the elimination of frills and services that are not essential to the basic program or activity. Difficulties arise because there is frequently disagreement on what constitutes a frill. This is perhaps the most vulnerable part of the planning and reporting process, for much energy can be used in defending or explaining why a certain activity is essential. Viewing

Transaction	Recorded in the Accounting Records in Month in Which			
	Order is placed	Materials are delivered	Materials are used	Check is issued
Placing an order for materials	As an obligation or encumbrance			
Materials delivered		As an accrued expenditure		
Materials used or consumed			As an applied cost (expense)	
Payment made for materials				As a disbursement of cash

Figure 5 Recording in the Accounting Record[12]

an activity in terms of the extent to which it furthers the objectives of the library in terms of benefits gained by the user is the purpose of assessment and may eliminate much of the discussion over what is and what is not a basic or needed service.

Information service, like many other professionally provided services, is only partially comprehended by funding agencies and by the public served. It is the responsibility of the information professional to show the value of the services provided.

EXPENDITURES

Expenditures are reported in a section separate from income. The form of expenditure reporting is dependent to an extent on the form of the budget. If a line-item budget is used, the reporting of expenditures will be by line item within each program, with general overhead such as administration, maintenance and utility costs reported separately.

There are four related steps in the expenditure process: appropriation, obligation or encumbrance, expenditure and disbursement. When an item of equipment, a book or a film is ordered, or services are contracted, there is an obligation or encumbrance against the particular item in the budget. Funds are obligated with the approval of a purchase order or the signing of a contract. As tax-supported organizations typically operate under an annual appropriation, such obligations are made so that they can be paid within the fiscal year. More funds are encumbered early in the fiscal year and the amount encumbered decreases as the year progresses. In some instances funds are made available on a quarterly basis. When this occurs, the pattern of encumbrance is adjusted accordingly. An encumbrance or obligation becomes an expenditure when goods and services are received along with a billing, and a disbursement is made.

Under accrual accounting, an expenditure and the liability or disbursement related to it is recorded when the goods and services are received. The purchase is recorded at the time of receipt of goods or services, not at the time of payment.

Liabilities are amounts owed as a result of expenditure activity. A contract with a book jobber is a liability, as is an order placed for a piece of furniture. Whatever is owed outside the organization is a liability. Long-term debts, such as those incurred for buildings or renovation, are usually recorded separately from the short-term liabilities within the general operating budget. This follows from the budgeting format, long-term special-purpose activities usually being part of the capital budget.

Disbursements are payments of cash for expenditures and occur at the time a check for payment is issued. If pre-payment is required, as for journal subscriptions, it is not a true expenditure until the goods or services are received, but is a loan. Although it should not be recorded as an expenditure until receipt of goods or services, most organizations record the expenditure upon payment.

The time period covered by reporting varies according to regulation and the use to which it is put. Internal reporting used to monitor activities is provided on a monthly basis. For policy-making bodies, it may be provided on a monthly or quarterly basis depending upon regulations and the frequency with which the bodies meet. Reports to funding authorities vary from monthly, to quarterly, to annual, again depending upon governing practices. Reporting to constituent groups and to the public is usually on an annual basis. In addition to regularly issued general statements of accounts, reports on specific funds or grants may be made at stated intervals. Reporting on the status of investments also may follow a schedule different from the monthly status of accounts. The capital budget is reported separately and typically less often than the operating budget unless there is unusual activity either in income or expenditure. Whatever differences there may be in reporting intervals, all budgets are reported annually and most are reported at least on a quarterly basis.

REPORTS AS EVALUATIVE TOOLS

Evaluating the way in which resources have been used and the resulting accomplishments is done in relation to the objectives of the organization. The objectives as stated in the long-range plan for the library are part of the program budget format. The objectives stated in those documents are the ones considered to be the most important to the organization. The budget is planned around and focused on them. The selection of reporting measures will be determined by the objectives.

In the planning process, objectives and the means for achieving them are chosen from among a number of possible alternatives. The means of achieving objectives are a best guess at a particular time, on the basis of available information. When data indicating level of accomplishment are available, it may become apparent that a different means of achieving the objective is now desirable. The reported data can then be used to justify program revision or a redirection of objectives. The use of evaluative data to monitor and revise program direction provides a constant feedback to the manager. This process is the basis of the planning/programming/budgeting systems. These systems include:

1) The consideration of alternative objectives and programs and, to the degree possible, careful definition of anticipated output and the resources necessary to achieve it.
2) The development of long-range multi-year programs.
3) A careful review of current output and costs of existing programs.
4) The comparison of alternative means of achieving objectives.

The planning, budgeting, reporting system is interactive, each step supporting the other and each potentially changing the others. The actual outcome of the planning effort which begins the budget cycle is known only as the activity moves toward completion.

In the planning process, priorities are set. Some of these have higher political visibility than others. Also, certain economic, political and environmental factors prevail. These may change as the budget year progresses and priorities may change accordingly. A special program may become too costly as it is implemented, utility charges or the cost of periodicals may increase beyond budgeted amounts, or other internal situations may occur that require a reallocation of resources. Most states and most institutions have regulations limiting internal transfers to five or ten per cent of the budget, but these limits can be raised with the approval of the governing body of the institution. In some institutions, there may be unwritten understandings that transfers from one item to another are acceptable. Such transfers are often from salary to operating lines; positions vacated during the year are not filled and the dollars are used elsewhere.

In a tax-supported institution, income does not increase over the year, and in some instances it may be reduced. State and municipal law includes safeguards against deficit spending and if revenues of the taxing body are reduced, impoundments on existing budgets can result. If revenues are uncertain, budgets can be frozen and certain types of expenditures may be prohibited. For these and other reasons, both political and economic, the budget that is approved may not be the budget that is actually implemented. The voter and the taxpayer have a right to know how their money was actually spent and what they got for it. The library manager has the responsibility to provide information. This, in its simplest terms, is what accountability is.

Managers have a fair amount of freedom in the manner in which they administer the budget once it is approved. This flexibility is necessary to enable the manager to respond to changing needs. If appropriately used, this flexibility permits the manager to reorder priorities, from those set by the tax-appropriating body to others that are more in line with changing demand. External controls on internal management are imposed to a greater or lesser degree dependent upon the political climate and the relationship between the funding authority and the library manager.

In responding to economic crises or reducing activity in a program that may have a high political priority but low institutional priority, managers have some internal discretion. This internal flexibility permits the manager to meet changing budget needs and to begin new projects which are exploratory or experimental. It also enables the manager to retain the status quo, for example by reducing funds for projects not initiated or welcomed by the library staff. An outreach program demanded by the community but that is less appealing to the library staff may be funded at a lower level than originally intended. If a program is of higher priority to library staff than to the funders, conversely, it may receive added funds. There is a social and political price to pay for such manipulation that counters public desire, and if the library manager rearranges priorities in this way, he or she must be willing to accept the consequences. If the library projects a customer-oriented attitude and then does not respond to customer needs, it must have very good reasons for such a course.

To a large extent, line-item budgets are the most easily manipulated in the above ways, as resources are allocated by item to the entire institution rather than to specific programs whose costs have been estimated.

The library manager can use external funds—those that are not part of the tax appropriation—in a number of ways to bolster programs of high library priority. New projects can be initiated and given a chance to become popular with the voters. Planning and early implementation can be carried out with funds from a federal or foundation grant and then the project can be transferred to the regular budget. This is often the thinking behind awards of planning grants—that the local funding authority will eventually assume long-term support of the resulting activity if it proves successful. A rather severe reaction to this has grown as state and local jurisdictions see this as a means of forcing additional support of the library. In a number of situations local jurisdictions have refused to accept planning money if the resulting program is to become part of their long-term financial responsibility. External funds can also be used for items that typically cause a controversy in the general operating budget, such as travel; if a travel cost can be built into federal or other grants it can be reduced elsewhere.

Criteria for evaluation are developed in advance of performance. They may be part of the legal requirements governing the organization, be established by the policy-making group, or designed to meet internal managerial needs. Criteria may also be set by user groups, related organizations, and the general public. As mentioned earlier, each of these is an audience for the reports issued by the organization and each has its own way of looking at and evaluating the library. Criteria to meet the evaluation requirements of these groups must be designed as carefully as the program whose output they measure.

Indicators—There are three levels of measurement of accomplishment: operations indicators, impact indicators and social indicators.

Operations indicators are output measures stating in non-financial terms what is produced as a result of the money and effort expended. They include workload measures and performance statistics such as circulation data, reference questions asked and answered, materials acquired, etc. Although they may be seen as outputs of specific departments, they are products of programs. These measures can be classified as volume indicators, quality indicators or comparative indicators. Responses to reference questions can be measured in each of these ways. The number of questions asked is a volume indicator; the volume answered promptly and accurately is an indicator of quality of service; the level of performance in relation to a prior year or in relation to a similar organization is a comparative indicator. Most operations indicators do not show the extent to which user needs are met. They show how much work is being done. Operations indicators usually consist of data that can be generated easily and are not necessarily comprehensive.

Program impact indicators are directly related to measuring the extent to which the program has met a public need. They are a combination of operations indicators within a program and are used to evaluate program performance against anticipated accomplishment. Although they are to a degree quantitative, there is a subjective element as well. The availability of reserve materials in a college library for a particular course may have enhanced the learning experience and improved the test scores of students taking the course, or the bibliographic instruction program may have increased the students' ability to use reference resources in support of course-related objectives. These outcomes can be measured to some extent, by a combination of subjective and objective operational indicators as they relate to an overall program.

Social indicators are even more general and reflect changes in overall social conditions that have resulted from the library activity. It is here that information service is justified as a public good. Is an informed electorate directly attributable to information service? Is research made possible by the resources of a library related to an improved quality of life? As the indicators become more general, they become increasingly difficult to quantify and to justify. The contribution of information service to the quality of life of the community it serves is a difficult but important question to answer.

Data, if they are to be evaluated objectively, must be both quantifiable and verifiable. The only indicators that meet these criteria are the operations indicators, but they may be related only to parts of programs and reflect attainment of only elements of stated objectives. For many library programs, there is no countable measure and there is little advantage in trying to force one. Studies have been done to determine the extent to which learning is increased if the library has open stacks, thus promoting browsability. Subjectively, librarians and other faculty members may be aware that the learning environment is improved in this fashion, but no set of objective measures is available.

Where qualifiable data are required, there may be an over-emphasis on the use of operations indicators. Library planners are justified in objecting that these data do not describe what an information service is or how well it is accomplishing its objectives.

Although attendance and circulation data are typically used to describe library activities, they are incomplete and misleading, but they have the virtues of being available, easy to obtain, and comparable with other libraries. As increased attention is devoted to developing outcome measures which are intended to quantify how information service enhances learning, or improves the community, we will begin to have measures that more directly answer the question, "Of what use is the library and its information services?"

Measures of Effectiveness—The specific measures of effectiveness that are used are collected from the records and reports of the parent agency as a general context, and specifically from the existing records of the library. These records are maintained in a form allowing interaction among the various elements of planning, budgeting, reporting and evaluation. The focus is both on the internal use of resources to meet program objectives and on the service provided to those who have the right to use it. The measures of effectiveness ideally meet the following criteria:[13]

1) Appropriateness and validity; does the measure relate to the objectives of library service and does it measure the extent to which the user's need is met?
2) Uniqueness; does it measure an aspect of the program not otherwise measured?
3) Completeness; does it measure most or all of the program objectives?
4) Comprehensiveness; is it understandable to the target group or groups?
5) Is the measure one that can be controlled internally or is it subject to external pressures? The cost of utilities is a factor of climate and the size of the utility bill is less a matter of good or poor management than it is of the state of the weather.
6) Is the cost of data collection worth the results?
7) Is the data collected disseminated in a timely fashion?
8) Is it accurate and reliable?

Measurement for evaluation has been a priority of all types of libraries in the past decade as it becomes increasingly important to justify all programs and the ways in which they are implemented. Declining budgets, increasing demand and an increasing complexity in the ways in which information service is delivered have all provided strong motivation to insure that our libraries and information services perform at peak efficiency and in support of the objectives of the larger communities of which they are a part.

Comparison with Like Organizations—Use of performance and financial data for comparison with other libraries or against general standards is an activity that should be conducted carefully and with a measure of skepticism. The more quantitative the information is, the less applicable it may be to the description and evaluation of the service it is supposed to measure. The development of benchmarking to allow for comparison among like agencies or activities or across time is equally as suspect in this regard as are data collected in earlier less sophisticated modes.

There is justification for a generalist approach in evaluating many library services, one involving more flexibility than the totally quantifiable approach. Tentative value judgments can then be made and priorities set with a recognition of both the quantifiable and non-quantifiable elements of information service considered. Under this approach, standards are seen as prevailing levels of service rather than as ways for measuring current objectives or performance in the local setting. The rejection of standards by many local governments is one of the reasons why ALA's Public Library Association moved from setting standards for public library service to developing a planning process which could be applied to local needs and interests, so that the development of local library service would be demonstrably responsive to the local situation. The professionals in any area, be they librarians, health care workers or public safety experts, tend to be suspect in the planning and evaluation process in that they tend to see their particular specialty as of first priority. The standards set by the professional associations to which they belong are seen by many government officials as unreasonably high, even self-serving.

The managers of a municipal government, an educational institution or a library have the responsibility to adapt the various standards to the needs of their particular environments. Standards also tend to be set on a functional rather than a program basis, and not all can be translated from one to another. This is another dimension of the problem of reconciling program requirements with quantifiable data.

SUMMARY

The purpose of financial reporting is to facilitate evaluation and decision-making by the various groups responsible for planning, budgeting and carrying out library programs. It is also a means of meeting the requirements for accountability to funding agencies, to client groups, and to the public.

Methods have been devised by accountants to meet standards of accounting practice, and these are often difficult for the uninitiated to understand. The need for accountability to the various constituencies, however, mandates that reporting, in addition to being accurate and objective, also be comprehensible. Information services are still poorly understood and little help in developing useful reporting systems for these services can be expected from accountants and management experts who are not knowledgeable in the field. Therefore, the development of responsive reporting systems is one that must be undertaken by the information profession itself.

NOTES

1. Emerson O. Henke, *Accounting for Nonprofit Organizations*. Belmont, Calif.: Wadsworth, 1977, p.1.
2. National Committee on Governmental Accounting, *Governmental Accounting, Auditing and Financial Reporting*. Chicago: Municipal Finance Officers Assn., 1968, p. 161.
3. Henke, p. 171
4. Henke, p. 172.
5. Thomas E. Steimer, "Activity-Based Accounting for Total Quality," *Management Accounting* 72:4, October, 1990, p. 39.
6. National Committee on Governmental Accounting, *Governmental Accounting, Auditing and Financial Reporting*. Chicago: Municipal Finance Officers Assn., 1968, pp. 106–126.
7. Daphne E. Kemperer and Barbara S. Shafer, "The Pilot Years, the Growth of the NACUBO Benchmarking Project," *NACUBO Business Officer* 27:6, December, 1993, p. 22.
8. Jack Traub, *Accounting and Reporting Practices for Private Foundations; A Critical Evaluation*. New York: Praeger, 1977, p.44.
9. Sidney Davidson, Clyde P. Stickney, and Roman L. Weil, *Inflation Accounting: A Guide for the Accountant and the Financial Analyst*. New York: McGraw-Hill, 1976, p.3.
10. *Ibid.*, p.15.

11. Adapted from *Frequently Asked Questions About Accrual Accounting in the Federal Government.* Washington, D.C.: General Accounting Office, 1970, p.5.

12. Davidson, p.15.

13. State-Local Finances Project, *Output Measures for a Multi-year Program and Financial Plan—PPB Note 7.* Washington D.C.: The George Washington University, 1967, p.9ff.

IX

A POSSIBLE FUTURE

The world of information and libraries has changed dramatically since the days of Benjamin Franklin. Where once libraries bought the important books and maintained collections of information for use by readers, they now also serve as access points to the whole world of information. In addition to serving as collectors and protectors of the written word, libraries now serve as nodes on networks which join libraries, government agencies, electronic journal publishers and many more information providers into an international information-access web. Where once a jurisdiction could state that it bought books to be used by its taxpayers and that use by others was not allowed, this is no longer possible to enforce in other than a very rudimentary manner.

Libraries have moved to the forefront in the information infra-structure that is being built. They have been leaders in developing networks which bring services available on the Internet to the library and through the library's services to the individual user. A farmer in Salisbury, Maryland can go to the public library and through a network developed by the state, with the support of federal funds, can access agricultural information residing in federal or other data bases, can check library catalogs, or can communicate with farmers with like concerns in the U.S. or abroad. From being collectors and protectors of information, librarians have become facilitators on the information highway, while at the same time continuing to provide traditional services.

ROLE OF PLANNING

In this new networked world of information, planning is of even greater importance than before. The external environmental forces which have an impact upon the creation, organization and delivery of information have increased in complexity. The availability of information in so many formats, so quickly, has affected the entire concept of what information service is, how it should be delivered, and who will pay for it. In the past fifty years we have moved from having limited information in some areas to a situation in which there is an excess of information in many areas: too much to identify, absorb, and act upon. The world of networked information has permitted the information user to amass a great deal of data and to manipulate it in a number of ways. Whether the information retrieved is the best or most useful information for the desired purpose is not always apparent.

Strategic planning has become an essential part of the activities of most organizations. The need to determine the present mission of the organization and to develop goals and objectives to achieve that mission provide a structured approach to service delivery. This is also a means of setting priorities for service which allows managers to apply funds to priority items. The increased popularity of Total Quality Management, which uses statistical data to support the planning process, has considerably sharpened the planning activity. Also, its emphasis on the customer provides a new focus to many organizations. In this mode, one would ask how providing network access enhances service to the customer and would seek some means of quantifying the level of satisfaction. This differs from earlier planning modes in which network access would be seen as a service to be made available to the customer but little or no effort would have been made to determine how satisfied the customer was with the service and what could be done to enhance that satisfaction. In the complex information world in which we now operate, the customer may be one of the few independent variables. Our planning may need to revolve around customer needs and how to satisfy them.

Local governments, educational institutions and other non-profit organizations within whose structures libraries and information services are located are developing new services which take advantage of the wealth of information available. As the new map of information access crosses governmental lines, new issues of who supports library service and who uses it become very confused. Most libraries are still firmly embedded in the book world even while reaching out electronically. Funders still see libraries with books, and individuals using those libraries, and therefore have something concrete to fund. As libraries move further into the electronic age, there will need to be redefinitions of service areas and their relation to tax support.

CHANGING VIEW OF PUBLIC GOOD

A basic tenet of library service and of the commitment to fund a substantial measure of that service is that it is a public good, something that goes beyond the limits of one organization or group in terms of the benefits that accrue. This belief has been questioned for some time. There is a perception among some political scientists that the concept of public good has led to an undue expansion of programs at government, and therefore taxpayers', expense. Thus a confrontation emerges. As health facilities, education, and libraries are among the services classified as public goods, and because they are highly labor-intensive, the professions from which employees for these services are drawn strongly resist any limitations in service. A coalition between client groups and those providing services develops and is highly resistant to changes that would reduce employment or service. The argument of opponents is that this creates a private benefit at public expense. Whether or not the strength of the client/professional coalition affects public expenditures and whether or not the politicization of the concept of public good skews it out of shape are issues that require review. Neither may be the case, but so long as these concerns exist among responsible planners and political scientists, they must be dealt with.

RESOURCE AVAILABILITY

The resources available to society to support all of its needs are limited. Rapid economic growth, a hallmark of earlier decades, has slowed, and the economy and the institutions it supports are growing at a much slower rate. With reduced resources, choices must be made of which services to fund and at what level. Over the past several years there has been a general feeling of reduced expectations and the need to adapt to a lower level of affluence. This is true both of individual expectations and expectations of the role of public services. In an economic environment in which growth is slow and in which many of the large industrial giants have found it necessary to reorganize and downsize their operations, hard choices must be made. Services which do not contribute to the economic and social welfare will not be funded. Libraries and information services must make a demonstrable contribution and must make both government and the citizen aware of this contribution. A factor in any sound planning process is the inclusion of those who will be affected by the decisions made. Support for information services is directly related to the degree to which those who are affected by the services are included in the decision-making process.

Sources of income for libraries vary with their clientele and their tax base. Public libraries have been and in the foreseeable future will continue to be supported in large part from local taxes. Local politicians talk about expanding the size of the group paying for local library services by including those in nearby areas who use those services. State officials on the other hand talk about the importance of local control. Each is looking elsewhere for funds to support local library service. Income from the various tax sources—property, sales, income—is lower on a per capita basis, while the costs of social services such as welfare and Medicare and the emphasis on public safety have increased. The support of education, libraries and related activities have much reduced resources at a time in which the information revolution is placing greater and more expensive demands on the services. Many cities have used up their capital of attractive buildings, good libraries and well-paved streets, and have had to invest in rebuilding or face further decline in the quality of life. Academic institutions grew rapidly in physical plant during the 1950s and 1960s and many of those buildings are in need of maintenance. Libraries which were built twenty or more years ago were not designed to meet the needs of the modern electronic information world. To be functional in the new world of information they must be able to function both as an electronic network node and as a place for the traditional interfaces between people and books.

A review of the tax base for libraries is in order. Numerous studies have indicated that the property tax as a source of local income has declined and that the effects of inflation on the cost of services has made local revenues even less able to meet needs. One response has been to change the size of the tax base, enlarging it to increase revenue. Library service is particularly well suited to a regional concept, as a linkage between a central library's resources and smaller library resource centers can provide better overall service and do so at no more cost than a number of small and often inadequate independent libraries that may lose users in any case to a larger better-equipped central library. Studies of spillover in use further support the efficacy of a broader tax base. The long-time independent public library and its board of trustees will be resistant but may eventually reach the conclusion that their choices are to consolidate funding or to slowly decline.

Realistically, in the next decade, any relief will be more likely to come through a redesign of local support, leading to consolidated services provided at a county or regional level. Achievement of such a reconfiguration will not be painless.

State-level support of library service has remained essentially the same for the past decade or more. Federal support of library service has barely held on in the past decade. Although categorical funding for libraries has continued in one form or another, the early days of strong support are gone. The emphasis has shifted at the federal level from libraries to investments in the information infrastructure. While libraries are part of this infrastructure, they are but one of many players. The development of inter-institutional teams to develop programs and provide information services is becoming increasingly popular. Partnering among libraries, community groups, outreach groups, local agencies and private industry to provide information services via the networks is a much more effective means of obtaining funds for information services than seeking federal funds for one library.

Because they are part of larger organizations, academic libraries are vulnerable in different ways to declining tax bases, mobility of populations, and public attitudes toward the service. The publicly supported institution, the private academic institution, and private associations of which libraries are a part are all vulnerable to those pressures. To the extent that they are subsidized by the local tax base, or are funded in part by the state through block or formula grants, that part of their income is directly vulnerable. The income from fees, tuition, foundations, investment returns and other private sources is also responsive to the economic health of the region or groups which serves as its primary support. A sensitivity to the economic health of the community providing support for library services is therefore crucial to an understanding of the forces likely to affect funding.

Financial planning is the process of identifying, allocating and accounting for resources necessary to carry out objectives. Without careful monitoring of the sources of income and the trends that affect those sources, libraries will find that other services and priorities, more sensitive to clientele and funding interests, will win in competing for support. The activities that most closely correlate with higher allocations are at the managerial level: research, planning and evaluation. The involvement of managers and policy makers is important to success in increasing funding.

TRENDS IN FINANCIAL MANAGEMENT

Library managers have become increasingly knowledgeable about ways of preparing information in support of library needs and indicating the effects of inflation on the cost of materials and on salaries. A broader view of the role of information service in the community, of what its purpose is and the extent to which the community can afford it, is needed. Concentrating on immediate funding difficulties is the narrow view and limits the directions the administrator can take in negotiating the library's fair share of the resources available from funding sources.

Library managers have become increasingly sophisticated both in the internal management of financial resources and in their external efforts to inform government and citizens of the value of information resources and services. One of the major directions in government over the past several years has been an increase in the professionalization of activities at all levels and this is likely to continue. The acquisition of business management skills is more and more a part of the preparation of those responsible for services. Long-range planning is now accepted as standard procedure by most organizations and this has served to develop an environment for management of resources that is based on an investigation of need and an analysis of capabilities. Systems review and analysis, another useful tool for planning and evaluation, has also become more commonly used in libraries.

The development of management information systems in libraries has provided important data on levels of activity and levels of expenditure and has allowed for continuous review and adjustment of the planning/budgeting documents. Libraries may have their own management systems or may share systems with the parent governing body. In either case, the system must be able to respond to the planning and reporting needs that are unique to library service as well as to areas of general concern.

The purpose of emphasis on the use of computer technology to organize and print out information in usable form, and on the continuous monitoring of the literature to identify additional ways of dealing with financial data, is to make better decisions concerning the ways in which financial resources can be located and allocated in response to stated objectives. Public sector goals tend to reflect broader client needs than do those in the private sector, and those goals tend to be less tangible. Some public sector services operate in a market situation and financial criteria are involved in the decision-making process: others are not provided on a fee-for-service basis. Libraries fall into both categories depending on their purpose, governance and policies, but most tend not to operate on a market basis.

Although financial constraints operate in both cases, they are less objective in those areas where there is no direct charge per unit of services. Cost-benefit then becomes a factor in decision-making, as does the concept of the public good of a service. Information services are varied in the clientele they serve and in the levels of service requested. Within a university, for example, the major library resource serves a teaching and research function for the entire campus and has goals and objectives derived from the parent institution. A research center may have a specialized information resource whose objectives are to support a particular project. Its purpose is different from that of the university library, and in overall planning considera-tion different criteria may need to be set. Similar considerations apply in municipal government where the public library's functions differ from that of a planning commission information resource or a historical archive.

Where profit cannot be used as a measure of performance, it is more difficult to allocate resources based on success of operation or demand for service. The expectation by the funding agency and by users of the service, that the service be accountable for the expendi-ture of funds and for providing a quality service, addresses this issue. As we identify outcomes assessment measures for library service, which look at what a student has learned or how a community has benefited economically from the information service provided, we will be increasingly able to demonstrate why libraries and informa-tion service are important.

Society has an increasing need for sophisticated information service. At the same time dollars needed to fund those services are declining and will continue to decline unless we rethink the ways in which the service is provided and is funded. If libraries are an integral part of the national information infrastructure, new national patterns of funding may emerge. But funding at the local level will still be necessary. Careful review of tax bases, fees for service and other income is necessary and is an important part of the financial package. Financial planning based on performance measurement in order to gain maximum return from resources is the goal of each library and information service.

SELECTED BIBLIOGRAPHY

Altman, Stanley M. "The Dilemma of Data Rich, Information Poor Public Service Organizations: Analyzing Operational Data," *Urban Analysis* 3:61–75 (1976).

Anthony, Robert N. *Financial Accounting in Non-Business Organizations.* Stamford, Conn.: Financial Accounting Standards Board, 1978.

Anthony, Robert N. and Regina Herzlinger. *Management Control in Non-Profit Organizations.* Homewood, Ill.: Richard D. Irwin, 1975.

Baldridge, J. Victor and Terrence E. Deal. *Managing Change in Educational Organizations.* Berkeley, Calif.: McCutchan, 1974.

Battin, Patricia. "New Ways of Thinking about Financing Information Services," in Brian L. Hawkins, ed. *Organizing and Managing Information Resources on Campus.* McKinney, TX: Academic Computing, Inc., 1989, pp. 369–383.

Bennett, Paul. *Up Your Accountability.* Washington, D.C.: The Taft Group, 1983.

Berger, Patricia. "An Investigation of the Relationship Between Public Relations Activities and Budget Allocation in Public Libraries," *Information Processing and Management* 15:179–193, (1979).

Bergeren, Peter M. and Lisa K. Miller. "Financial Statement Analysis, the Research Process in a Business Library," *Journal of Business and Finance Librarianship,* 1:4, 1993, pp. 49–59.

Berke, Richard L. "Pragmatism Guides Political Gifts, A Study Shows," *New York Times,* 139:48, 360, Sept. 16, 1990, p. 26.

Bevan, R. G. "Management for Evaluation," *Omega* 8:311–321 (1980).

Borst, Diane and Patricia J. Montana. *Managing Nonprofit Organizations.* New York: Amacom, 1977.

Burns, William J., Jr., and Don T. DeCoster. *Accounting and Its Behavioral Implications.* New York: McGraw-Hill, 1969.

Burton, Richard M. and Børge Obel. "The Efficiency of the Price, Budget and Mixed Approaches Under Varying a Priori Information Levels for Decentralized Planning," *Management Science* 26:401–417 (April 1980).

Button, K. J. "Models for Decision-Making in the Public Sector," *Omega* 7:399–409 (1979).

Christianson, Ellory. "Depreciation of Library Collections: A Matter of Interpretation," *Library Administration and Management* 6:1, Winter, 1992, p. 41.

———. *Chronicle of Higher Education* 40:20, January 19, 1994, p. A34.

Council of State Governments. *Zero Base Budgeting in the States.* Lexington, Ky.: The Council, 1976.

Cowing, Thomas and A. G. Holtman. *The Economics of Local Public Service Consolidation.* Lexington, Mass.: Heath, 1976.

Davidson, Sidney, Clyde P. Stickney, and Roman L. Weil. *Inflation Accounting: A Guide for the Accountant and the Financial Analyst.* New York: McGraw-Hill, 1976.

Dayton, Allan S. "Operations Auditing Answers Questions Beyond the Scope of Financial Reports," *Management Controls* 24:21–215 (September–October 1977).

Deardon, John. "Cost Accounting Comes to Service Industries," *Harvard Business Review* 56:132–140 (September–October 1978).

Derber, Milton and Martin Wagner. "Public Sector Bargaining and Budget Making Under Fiscal Adversity," *Industrial and Labor Relations Review* 33:18–23 (October 1979).

Dickson, G. W. and John K. Simmons. "The Behavioral Side of MIS; Some Aspects of the 'People Problem.'" *Business Horizons* 13:59–71 (August 1970).

Drake, Miriam A. "Attribution of Library Costs." *College and Research Libraries* 38:514–519 (November 1977).

Drinan, Helen. "Financial Management of Online Services—A How-to Guide," *ONLINE* 3:14–21 (October 1979).

Fisher, Gene H. *Cost Considerations in Systems Analysis.* New York: American Elsevier, 1971.

Forrester, John P. "Municipal Capital Budgeting: An Examination," *Public Budgeting and Finance,* 13:2 Summer, 1993, p. 92.

Francl, Thomas J., W. Thomas Linn, and Miklos Vasarhelyi. "ZBB Fits DP to a TEE," *Datamation* 26:177–180 (September 1980).

Friedman, Lewis B. *Budgeting Municipal Expenditures, a Study in Comparative Policy Making.* New York: Praeger, 1975.

Gregory, Geoffrey. "Cash Flow Models: A Review," *Omega* 4:643–656 (1976).

Gross, Malvern J. and Wm. Wardshauer. *Financial and Accounting Guide for Nonprofit Organizations,* 3rd ed. New York: Wiley, 1979.

Hale, George E. and Scott R. Douglass, "The Politics of Budget Execution, Financial Manipulation in State and Local Government," *Administration and Society* 9:367–378 (November 1977).

Hartman, Robert W. "Next Steps in Budget Reform: Zero Base Review and the Budgeting Process," *Policy Analysis* 3:387–394 (Summer 1977).

Hatry, Harry, "The Alphabet Soup Approach: You'll Love It," *The Public Manager,* 21:4, Winter, 1992–93, p. 9.

Hatry, Harry P., Louis H. Blair, Donald M. Fisk, John H. Grenier, John R. Hall, Jr., Philip S. Schaenman. *How Effective Are Your Community Services? Procedures for Monitoring the Effectiveness of Municipal Services?* Washington, D.C.: The Urban Institute and the International City Managers Association, 1977.

Henke, Emerson O. *Accounting for Nonprofit Organizations.* Belmont, Calif.: Wadsworth, 1977.

Herbert, Bernard P. *Modern Public Finance.* Homewood, Ill.: Richard D. Irwin, 1979.

Hertschke, Gilbert C. and Ellen Kehoe. "Serial Acquisition as a Capital Budgeting Program," *Journal of the American Society for Information Science* 31:5, September, 1980, p. 357.

Heyeck, John C., ed. *Managing Under Austerity, A Conference for Privately Supported Academic Libraries.* Stanford, Calif.: Stanford University, 1976.

Heyel, Carl. *The VNR Concise Guide to Accounting and Control* (VNR Concise Management Series). New York: Van Nostrand, 1979.

Hills, Frederick S. and Thomas S. Mahoney. "University Budgets and Organizational Decision Making," *Administrative Science Quarterly* 23:454–465 (September 1978).

Holtman, A. G., T. Tabsz, and W. Kruse. "The Demand for Local Public Services, Spillovers, and Urban Decay: The Case of Public Libraries," *Public Finance Quarterly* 4:97–113 (January 1976).

Hoover, Ryan E. "Computer Aided Reference Services in the

Academic Library; Experiences in Organizing and Operating an On Line Reference Service," *ONLINE* 3:28–40 (October 1979).

Hopkins, David S. P. "Computer Models Employed in University Administration: The Stanford Model," *Interfaces* 9:13–22 (February 1979).

Houck, Lewis D. *A Practical Guide to Budgetary and Management Control Systems.* Lexington, Mass.: Heath, 1979.

House, Peter W. and Robert G. Ryan. *The Future Indefinite; Decision Making in a Transition Economy.* Lexington, Mass.: Heath, 1979.

International City Managers Assn. *Municipal Finance Administration.* 6th ed. Chicago: The Assn., 1962.

Jones, Reginald L. and George H. Trentin. *Budgeting: Key to Planning and Control.* New York: American Management Assn., 1971.

Kahn, Herman and John B. Phelps. "The Economic Present and Future: A Chartbook for the Decade Ahead," *The Futurist* 13:203–222 (June 1979).

Kaud, Faisal A. "Operating Budgets Are Valuable in Managing Finances," *Hospitals: Journal of the American Hospital Assn.* 51:69–73 (November 16, 1977).

Kemerer, Frank R. and Ronald Satryb. *Facing Financial Exigency, Strategies for Educational Administration.* Lexington, Mass.: Lexington Books, 1977.

Kempner, Daphne E. and Barbara S. Shafer. "The Pilot Years, the Growth of the NACOBO Benchmarking Project," *NACOBO Business Officer,* 27:6, December, 1993, pp. 21–31.

Kenis, Izzettin. "Effects of Budgetary Goal Characteristics on Managerial Attitudes and Performance," *The Accounting Review* 54:707–721 (October 1979).

Keown, Arthur J. and John D. Martin. "Capital Budgeting in the

Public Sector: A Zero-one Goal Programming Approach," *Financial Management* 7:21–26 (Summer 1978).

Kristensen, Ole P. "The Logic of Political-Bureaucratic Decision Making as a Cause of Governmental Growth," *European Journal of Political Research* 8:249–264 (1980).

Lee, Hwa-Wei and Gary A. Hunt. *Fundraising for the 1990s: The Challenge Ahead.* Canfield, Ohio: Genaway, 1992.

Lesher, R. Schuyler and Edward J. Mazur. "A New Approach to an Old Problem: How to Implement a Financial Accounting System in a University," *Management Focus* 27:15–21 (March–April 1980).

Littleton, Isaac T. *State Systems of Higher Education and Libraries: A Report for the Council on Library Resources.* Raleigh, N.C.: N.C. State University, November 1977.

McCarty, William E. "An Entity—Relationship View of Accounting Models," *The Accounting Review* 54:667–686 (October 1979).

Maier, Joan M. "The Three Deadly C's—Cost, Copyright, and aCcounting," *ONLINE* 3:61–63 (October 1979).

Martin, Murray S. *Budgetary Control in Academic Libraries.* Greenwich, Conn.: JAI Press, 1978.

Martin, Murray S., ed. Library Finance: New Needs, New Models, *Library Trends* (Urbana, Ill.: University of Illinois) 42:3, Winter, 1994.

Mason, Robert M. "A Lower Bound Cost Benefit Model for Information Services," *Information Processing and Management* 14:71–83 (1978).

Massey, William F. "A Dynamic Equilibrium Model for University Budget Planning." *Management Science* 23:248–256 (November 1976).

Massey, William F. and Joel W. Meyerson, eds. *Strategy and Finance in Higher Education.* Princeton, N.J.: Peterson's Guides, 1992.

Mautz, Robert K. "Inflation Accounting: Which Method Is Best?" *Management Review* 66:11–17 (November 1977).

Minmier, George S. *An Evaluation of the Zero Base Budgeting System in Governmental Institutions.* (Schools of Business Administration Monograph #68.) Athens, Ga.: Georgia State University, 1975.

Mitchell, Betty Jo, Norman E. Tanis and Jack Jaffe. *Cost Analysis of Library Functions; A Total Systems Approach.* Greenwich, Conn.: JAI Press, 1978.

Moore, Perry. "Zero-Base Budgeting in American Cities," *Public Administration Review* 40:253–258 (May/June 1980).

Morton, James R. "Qualitative Objectives of Financial Accounting: A Comment on Relevance and Understandability," *Journal of Accounting Research* 12:288–298 (Autumn 1974).

Murphy, Richard C. "A Computer Model Approach to Budgeting," *Management Accounting* 56:34–39 (June 1975).

Nathan, Richard P., Allen D. Marvel, Susannah E. Calkins, and Associates. *Monitoring Revenue Sharing.* Washington, D.C.: The Brookings Institute, 1975.

National Center for Educational Studies. *Public Libraries in the United States: 1991.* Washington, D.C.: U.S. Department of Education, Office of Research and Improvement, 1993, p. 36.

Neumann, Seev and Eli Segev. "Evaluate Your Information System," *Journal of Systems Management* 31:34–41 (March 1980).

Newbould, Gerald D. "A Catastrophe Theory Analysis: City Government Finances," *Public Finance Quarterly* 8:307–321 (July 1980).

Niland, Powell. "Developing Standards for Library Expenditures," *Management Science* 13:797–808 (August 1967).

Ochs, Jack. *Public Finance.* New York: Harper and Row, 1974.

Orleans, Harold, ed. *Nonprofit Organizations; A Government Management Tool.* New York: Praeger, 1980.

Osborne, David and Ted Gaebler. *Reinventing Government: How the Entrepreneurial Spirit Is Transforming the Public Sector.* Reading, Mass.: Addison-Wesley, 1992.

Oster, Gary. "Local Business May Have Money for the Asking," *American Libraries* 11:373–377 (June 1980).

Oxenfeldt, Alfred R. *Cost-Benefit Analysis for Executive Decision Making; The Danger of Plain Common Sense.* New York: American Management Assn., 1979.

Patillo, James W. *Zero-Base Budgeting, A Planning, Resource Allocation and Control Tool.* New York: National Assn. of Accountants, 1977.

Price, Douglas S. "Rational Cost Information: Necessary and Obtainable," *Special Libraries* 65:49–57 (February 1974).

Rachlen, Robert. *Handbook of Budgeting, Third Edition.* New York: Wiley, 1993.

Radford, K. J. *Complex Decision Problems; An Integrated Strategy for Resolution.* Reston, Va.: Reston Publishing Co., 1977.

Raisheck, Gordon. "How the Choice of Measures of Effectiveness Constrains Operational Analysis," *Interfaces* 9:85–93 (August 1979).

Rose, Howard. *Financial Statements, A Crusade for Current Values.* Toronto: Sir Isaac Pitman Ltd., 1969.

Rosenthal, Stephen R. "Managing the Demand for Public Service Delivery Systems: Anticipation, Diagnosis and Program Response," *Urban Analysis* 6:15–31 (1979).

Ryan, Joseph E. "Profitability in a Non-Profit Environment," *Journal of Systems Management* 31:6–12 (August 1980).

Said, K. E. "A Goal Oriented Budgetary Process," *Management Accounting* 56:31–36 (January 1975).

Savich, Richard S. "The Use of Accounting Information in Decision Making," *The Accounting Review* 52:642–657 (July 1977).

Savich, Richard S. and Keith B. Ehrenreich. "Cost/Benefit Analysis of Human Resource Accounting Alternatives," *Human Resource Management* 15:7–18 (Spring 1976).

Sharansky, Ira. *The Politics of Taxing and Spending.* Indianapolis: Bobbs-Merrill, 1969.

Sherr, Lawrence A. and Deborah J. Teeter. *Total Quality Management in Higher Education.* San Francisco: Jossey-Bass, 1991.

Shih, Wei. "A General Decision Model for Cost-Volume-Profit Analysis Under Uncertainty," *The Accounting Review* 54:687–706 (October 1979).

Shoemaker, Thomas P. *Public Library Automation Network; A Cost/Benefit Analysis of the PLAN Project.* Sacramento: California State Library, 1977.

Slavet, Joseph S., Katherine L. Bradbury, Philip Moss. *Financing State-Local Services: A New Strategy for Greater Equity.* Lexington, Mass.: D. C. Heath, 1975.

Smith Craig. "Mixing Oil and Water: The New Partnerships Between Foundations and Government," *Foundation News* 21:25–31 (December 1980).

Smith, Steven R. and Michael Lipsky. *Nonprofits for Hire; The Welfare State in the Age of Contracting.* Cambridge, MA.: Harvard University Press, 1993.

Sorensen, James E. and Hugh D. Grove. "Cost-Outcome and Cost-Effectiveness Analysis: Emerging Nonprofit Performance Evaluation Techniques," *The Accounting Review* 52:658–675 (July 1977).

Spiro, Herbert T. *Finance for the Non-Financial Manager.* New York: Wiley, 1977.

Steimer, Thomas E. "Activity Based Accounting for Total Quality," *Management Accounting.* 72:4, October, 1990, pp. 39–42.

Stovich, Paul J. *Zero-Base Planning and Budgeting; Improved Cost Control and Resource Allocation.* Homewood, Ill.: Dow-Jones-Irwin, 1977.

Swieringa, Robert J. "A Behavioral Approach to Participative Budgeting," *Management Accounting* 56:35–39 (February 1975).

Taulhee, Richard K. "The CPE Industry," *The Ohio CPA Journal* 48:4, Winter, 1989, p. 53.

Tomer, Christinger. "The Effects of the Recession on Academic and Public Libraries," *The Bowker Annual; 37th Edition.* New Providence, N.J.: Bowker, 1992, pp. 77–78.

Traub, Jack. *Accounting and Reporting Practices of Private Foundations; A Critical Evaluation.* New York: Praeger, 1977.

Tsaklanganos, Angelos A. "Sense and Nonsense in Financial Reporting by Nonprofit Organizations," *MSU Business Topics* 27:25–33 (Winter 1979).

Turk, Frederick J. "Cost Behavior Analysis: A Road Map of the Uncertain Future," *Management Controls* 24:17–20 (September–October 1977).

van Dam, Cees, ed. *Trends in Managerial and Financial Accounting.* Boston: Martinus Nijhoff Social Sciences Division, 1978.

Vatter, William J. *Operating Budgets.* Belmont, Calif.: Wadsworth, 1969.

Virginia Beach Dept. of Public Libraries. *Cost/Benefit Analysis of a Catalog System for the Virginia Beach Dept. of Public Libraries.* Virginia Beach, Va.: The Department, January 1978.

West, Richard P. "Library Budgets: Re-orienting Where We Spend Our Money," *Cause/Effect* 17:2, Summer, 1994, p. 3.

Whalen, Edward L. *Responsibility Center Budgeting.* Bloomington, Ind.: Indiana University Press, 1991.

White, Herbert S. "Cost-Effectiveness and Cost-Benefit Determinations in Special Libraries," *Special Libraries* 70:163–169 (April 1979).

Wildavsky, Aaron. *The Politics of the Budgetary Process.* Boston: Little, Brown, 1964.

Williams, Martin. "The Impact of Revenue Sharing Funds on Local Expenditures," *Urban Analysis* 6:49–58 (1979).

Wilson, John H., Jr. "Costs, Budgeting and Economics of Information Processing," *Seventh Annual Review of Information Science and Technology.* Washington, D.C.: American Society for Information Science, 1972, pp. 39–67.

Worthley, John A. and William G. Ludwin. *Zero Base Budgeting in State and Local Government; Current Experiences and Cases.* New York: Praeger, 1979.

INDEX

ABOUT THE AUTHOR

Ann Prentice is both a practitioner in the area of financial planning and a student of the subject. She has been a public library director, public library trustee, and system trustee. She has conducted research and written three books and numerous articles on the subject, and has consulted widely in this area both with library staffs and with agencies conducting research on topics related to financing libraries and information centers. Her undergraduate degree is in political science from the University of Rochester (N.Y.). She holds the MLS from SUNY-Albany and her doctorate in Library/Information Science from Columbia University. She is currently the Dean of the College of Library and Information Services at the University of Maryland. She is past president of the American Society for Information Science and of the Association for Library and Information Science Education.